NUGGETS

Short Stories for Personal Management

Sunil Thomas, Ph.D.

SUNIPRINT

A Division of Abraham Thomas Foundation

NUGGETS
Short Stories for
Personal Management

Copyright © Sunil Thomas/SUNIPRINT
2024

Cover Design: Sunil Thomas

ISBN: 979-8-9866300-9-0

SUNIPRINT
A Division of Abraham Thomas Foundation
11 Cambridge Road, Broomall, PA-19008, USA
E-mail: suniprintbooks@gmail.com

TABLE OF CONTENTS

PREFACE 5
1. YOUR LIFE IS LEAD BY YOUR MISSION .7
2. GLASS CEILING 12
3. TROPICAL FOREST, SWAMP AND DESERT 15
4. WARDING OFF AN ATTACK 18
5. THE WORLD IS A STAGE, PLAY IT RIGHT 21
6. PERIPHERAL VICES 24
7. THE JOURNEY 26
8. ENVIRONMENT 28
9. THE RACE 30
10. TRANSFORMATION 32
11. THE WEIGHT OF POWER 34
12. THE ERA 36
13. DEEP CLEANING 40
14. MAKING A FOOL OF ONESELF 42
15. STANDING OUT AMONGST THE CROWD 44
16. UNDER PRESSURE 46
17. BREAKING THE VICE 48
18. THE HEAVENLY BUTTERFLY 51
19. THE BROKER 53
20. FINANCIAL DISCIPLINE 56
21. THE SHIRT 59
22. PRIORITY 61
23. MAINTAIN A SHARP BRAIN THROUGHOUT LIFE 62
24. ADAPTABILITY 64
25. DYSBIOTIC POPULACE 67
26. THE RUBIK'S CUBE 69

27. WORTH OF A DIAMOND 72
28. LABOR OF LOVE...............................74
29. THE MOST VALUABLE TIME................77
30. THE CONTAINER 80
31. THE RACE TRACK 82
32. ONE KEY PIANO 84
33. REMEBERING YOU 86
34. THE POWERLESS GOD 88
35. PARTY TO A CRIME 91
36. SHADOW OF DEATH............................94
37. OVERCOMING CHALLENGES 96
38. RETIREMENT 98
39. THE CRITIQUE....................................101
40. THE FAÇADE OF WEALTH..................103
41. THE EARTHLY LIFE 106
42. LIVING FOR OTHERS 109
43. ASSAULTING THE SPEAKER..............111
44. EXTRAVAGANT SPENDING OF TIME 114
45. TRANSFER OF WEALTH 116
46. THE PRIORITY OF MAN CHANGES EVERY TEN YEARS.............................119
47. CHANGE OF GUARD 121
48. CONFRONTING ADVERSITY 123
49. THE LEMONADE SELLER 126
50. STRATEGIC LEADERSHIP IN GOVERNANCE: LESSONS FROM A VICE CHANCELLOR..129
51. NAVIGATING LIFE'S POTHOLES 132
52. STAYING RELEVANT...........................134
53. DEFINING FACTORS 137
54. THE SUCCESSFUL CEO IN THE BOARDROOM 140
55. WORKING EFFORTLESSLY.................143

56. ANERGIC BEHAVIOR IS DETRIMENTAL TO STUDENTS, WORKERS AND EXECUTIVES 146
57. EXPERIENCE MATTERS 149
58. PASSION TRIUMPHS 152
59. TRANSITIONING TO RETIREMENT YEARS 155
60. IF YOU DO NOT LEAD YOUR LIFE, YOU WILL SURRENDER TO OTHERS 157
61. PROSPERITY THROUGH INDIVIDUAL CONTRIBUTION 159
62. THE GOLD NUGGET 161
63. BETTER STAY LONELY AT THE TOP THAN IN THE DITCH 164
64. IMPORTANCE OF CONTINUING EDUCATION 166
65. ZERO TO HERO 168
66. RESURRECTING GRANDEUR 171
67. PREDICTING YOUR HEALTH USING AI 175
68. THE SURPRISE AT THE BATTLEFIELD 179
69. YOUR WORK TOUCH MANY LIVES THAT YOU ARE NOT AWARE 183
70. TAKING THE INITIATIVE 187
71. THE JUDGE 190
72. CULTIVATING PERSONAL GROWTH . 195
73. LONGEVITY OF AN ACCOMPLISHMENT 199
74. LESSER KNOWN HABITS CAN TOPPLE US 203
75. PRACTICE 205
76. UNDERCURRENTS 208

77. JACK OF SEVERAL TRADES 212
78. CALMING THE STORMS IN OUR LIVES
.... 215
79. REPENTANCE AND RENEWAL AT
EASTER 218
80. THE SANTA CLAUS 220

PREFACE

Personal management is the process of efficiently managing your life and career to achieve your goals and contribute meaningfully to your personal and professional environments. It involves setting clear objectives, organizing your time and resources, and maintaining a balance between various aspects of your life.

We all encounter challenges in life, whether they are related to our careers, personal relationships, health, or finances. Personal management equips us with the skills and strategies needed to navigate these challenges effectively.

Personal management helps you set and achieve your goals, manage time efficiently, develop organizational skills, maintain work-life balance, improve communication, foster personal growth, build resilience.

In addition to these traditional challenges, we are also facing modern issues like climate change and automation. Personal management is crucial in helping us navigate these complexities. By developing a proactive approach to these global challenges, we can adapt our skills, make informed decisions, and contribute to sustainable solutions.

By mastering personal management, you can significantly enhance your overall well-being, ensuring that you maintain a healthy balance between various aspects of your life. This involves managing stress effectively, cultivating a positive mindset, and making time for activities that promote physical and mental health. As a result, you become more resilient, better equipped to handle life's challenges, and more fulfilled in your personal and professional endeavors.

Achieving your aspirations becomes more attainable as you develop the skills to set clear, actionable goals and create structured plans to reach them. Efficient time management, prioritization, and organizational skills allow you to make steady progress toward your dreams, whether they are career-related or personal. This systematic approach helps you stay focused and motivated, turning ambitions into tangible achievements.

This book, Nuggets, provides short stories on personal management. The stories offer practical insights and real-life examples that may be helpful in developing your personal management skills and strategies.

1. YOUR LIFE IS LEAD BY YOUR MISSION

Leading a life guided by your mission implies that you possess a well-defined purpose or goal that serves as a guiding principle in everything you do. This mission becomes the driving force behind your actions, decisions, and aspirations, profoundly shaping the trajectory of your life.

When your life is governed by a mission, it means you have a clear sense of direction and focus. You are not wandering aimlessly; instead, you have a purpose that imbues your existence with meaning and significance. This mission acts as a compass, providing you with a sense of purpose and fulfillment as you navigate the myriad challenges and opportunities life presents.

Having a mission instills within you a deep sense of passion and determination. It fuels your ambition and propels you to pursue your goals with unwavering dedication and perseverance. Despite encountering obstacles and setbacks, your unwavering commitment to your mission empowers you to overcome adversity and attain success.

Moreover, when your life is guided by your mission, you are more inclined to make decisions that align with your values and aspirations. You become deliberate in how you

7

allocate your time, energy, and resources, prioritizing activities and endeavors that contribute to the realization of your mission.

Living a life driven by your mission also cultivates a profound sense of fulfillment and satisfaction. As you actively work towards something meaningful and impactful, you experience a deep sense of purpose and joy. Each milestone achieved and obstacle overcome reinforces your sense of accomplishment and strengthens your dedication to your mission.

Furthermore, a life led by your mission often transcends personal fulfillment to encompass making a positive impact on others and the world at large. Your mission may involve serving others, contributing to your community, or effecting change in society. By living in alignment with your mission, you become a catalyst for positive transformation and inspire others to pursue their own passions and purposes.

Maintaining a balance between your professional aspirations and your familial responsibilities can be particularly challenging when driven by a mission. The demands of your career may necessitate significant time and energy, potentially leading to conflicts with your family commitments. Juggling long work hours, travel obligations, and the pursuit of ambitious goals with quality time spent with loved ones can strain relationships and create tension within the family unit.

The sacrifices required to remain steadfast in your mission can impact your family life. This may involve missing significant milestones, such as birthdays or family gatherings, or prioritizing work commitments over personal time with your spouse or children. Navigating these competing priorities necessitates careful communication, compromise, and a robust support system to ensure that both your professional and family life thrive.

In your professional life, being mission-oriented entails a steadfast dedication to achieving specific goals or making a meaningful impact in your chosen field. This often entails confronting obstacles such as intense competition, resource limitations, and unforeseen setbacks. Whether striving for career advancement, launching a new business venture, or pursuing a passion project, the journey towards success is rarely straightforward.

Moreover, the pursuit of a mission-oriented life can sometimes engender feelings of isolation or loneliness, especially if your objectives set you apart from societal norms or necessitate challenging conventional wisdom. You may encounter skepticism or resistance from others who do not share your vision, underscoring the importance of cultivating a supportive network of like-minded individuals who can offer encouragement and guidance along the way.

Despite these challenges, embracing a mission-oriented life can yield immense fulfillment and satisfaction. When you are propelled by a sense of purpose and guided by your core values, every obstacle becomes an opportunity for growth and learning. The resilience and determination required to surmount these hurdles ultimately fortify your character and deepen your commitment to your mission.

Involving your family in your mission can foster a sense of shared purpose and unity, transforming challenges into opportunities for bonding and mutual support. By aligning your professional pursuits with your family's values and aspirations, you can forge a harmonious balance that enriches both aspects of your life. Living a mission-driven life becomes a collaborative journey, strengthening both your career and familial relationships, and allowing you to achieve a holistic sense of success and fulfillment.

Ultimately, a mission-driven life not only elevates your personal and professional achievements but also creates a ripple effect of positive influence on those around you. As you pursue your mission with passion and integrity, you inspire others to discover and follow their own paths, contributing to a more purposeful and interconnected world.

2. GLASS CEILING

Alain had a deep passion for plants that extended far beyond mere interest. His enthusiasm led him to explore every park and garden within his state, and even those in the neighboring states. His botanical adventures took him to various locations, each offering unique flora and lush landscapes.

One memorable visit was to an expansive greenhouse nestled within a grand garden. This greenhouse was a marvel of engineering and horticulture, featuring a wide array of plant species from different climates. Alain was particularly captivated by the section dedicated to tropical trees. These trees, with their towering presence and broad leaves, created an exotic and verdant environment within the greenhouse.

However, due to their impressive height, the caretakers had to regularly trim the tops of these tropical giants to prevent them from breaking through the glass ceiling. This careful pruning ensured that the greenhouse remained intact while still allowing visitors to appreciate the majesty of the trees. The experience left Alain in awe of the balance between nature's grandeur and human ingenuity in maintaining such a delicate yet breathtaking display.

We construct an invisible glass ceiling above us, a barrier shaped by our values and priorities. This self-imposed limit influences our aspirations and defines the boundaries of what we believe we can achieve. The glass ceiling is not a physical barrier but a psychological one, stemming from our internal beliefs, societal norms, and the priorities we set in our lives.

Our values, the principles that guide our decisions, play a crucial role in determining the height of this ceiling. When we prioritize security and comfort over growth and challenge, we might unknowingly lower our ceiling, restricting our potential. Conversely, when we value ambition, innovation, and resilience, we elevate this ceiling, unlocking greater possibilities and achievements.

Recognizing the nature of this ceiling is essential. Though transparent and seemingly invisible, it is also fragile. With the right mindset and actions, it can be shattered. By reassessing our values and realigning our priorities, we can break through this glass ceiling, transcending the limitations we have unconsciously set for ourselves.

This glass ceiling serves as both a reflection of and a constraint on our potential. It reminds us that the only true limits are those we impose upon ourselves. By daring to question and redefine our values and priorities, we can dismantle this ceiling and reach heights we once thought unattainable.

In essence, the glass ceiling symbolizes the power of self-perception and the impact of our choices. It challenges us to look inward, examine the principles that govern our lives, and make conscious decisions to foster growth and achievement. By doing so, we not only break free from our self-imposed limitations but also inspire others to recognize and overcome their own barriers.

3. TROPICAL FOREST, SWAMP AND DESERT

After completing his studies, Jose immigrated to a foreign country to start a job in a large organization. Upon arriving, he diligently familiarized himself with the rules and regulations related to immigration, as well as the various services offered by both the city and his organization. His thorough understanding of these systems made him a valuable resource for new immigrants who sought his advice and guidance.

Jose quickly became known for his willingness to help others navigate the complexities of settling in a new country. His door was always open, and many new arrivals found solace in his knowledge and experience. One such individual was Dave, a fellow immigrant who frequently sought Jose's counsel.

On one occasion, Dave expressed his gratitude in a heartfelt manner, saying to Jose, "Every time I come to you, I feel like I arrive empty-handed. But after our conversations, I leave rich, laden with invaluable information." This sentiment encapsulated the profound impact Jose had on those around him, highlighting his role as a beacon of support and wisdom in the immigrant community.

People can often be compared to two distinct types: those resembling a Tropical Forest and those akin to a Desert. Individuals who are like the Tropical Forest are known for their generosity and willingness to help anyone who seeks their assistance. They go out of their way to support others, offering guidance, resources, and a listening ear without expecting anything in return. Their presence is refreshing and nurturing, much like the lush, abundant environment of a tropical forest that sustains diverse life.

On the other hand, there are those whose personalities are comparable to a Desert. These individuals tend to be indifferent or unhelpful. They do not go out of their way to assist others and often remain detached and unresponsive to the needs around them. However, even within the desert category, there are variations. Some people are like a cold desert—aloof and distant, providing no warmth or comfort. Others are akin to a hot desert, where their indifference is paired with an overwhelming intensity, making interactions with them feel draining and uncomfortable.

Additionally, there are personalities that resemble Swamps. These individuals might initially seem helpful or approachable, but there is a hidden catch. When you seek their advice or assistance, they end up soliciting services or favors from you in return. Instead of receiving the help you sought, you find yourself entangled in their demands, much like how a swamp ensnares anything that enters its murky waters.

In summary, people's personalities can be as diverse as natural landscapes—some are nurturing like tropical forests, some are indifferent like deserts, and others are deceptively entangling like swamps. Understanding these differences can help navigate interactions and set expectations accordingly.

4. WARDING OFF AN ATTACK

In the untamed wilderness of Asia's dense jungles or the vast plains of Africa, the timeless struggle between predator and prey unfolds with raw intensity. Here, amidst the tangled undergrowth or beneath the scorching sun, the intricate dance of life and death plays out against a backdrop of primal instincts and unforgiving landscapes.

In the heart of Africa, the majestic lions reign supreme as the apex predators of the savanna. With sinewy muscles rippling beneath their golden coats, they stalk their formidable prey with silent determination. Among their favored targets are the imposing Cape buffaloes, massive beasts whose strength and resilience rival that of their feline adversaries.

In the heat of the chase, the lions employ cunning tactics to bring down their quarry. One may leap onto the buffalo's back, its powerful jaws clamping down with lethal precision, while another may seize hold of its neck, seeking to immobilize the massive creature with a vice-like grip. Yet, the Cape buffaloes are no easy prey. With thunderous hooves and lethal horns, they unleash a ferocious counterattack, their formidable defenses capable of inflicting grievous harm upon their assailants.

In this deadly game of cat and mouse, strength and strategy are equally matched. The lions, though mighty hunters, must navigate a perilous dance with their quarry, knowing that a single misstep could spell their doom. And so, they bide their time, exerting their dominance with calculated precision, yet ever wary of the Cape buffaloes' formidable defenses.

In the relentless arena of the unforgiving wilderness, the delicate equilibrium of power is in perpetual flux. As the lions grow weary from their tireless pursuit, the Cape buffaloes seize upon the opportune moment, mounting an assault that forces their would-be predators into a hasty retreat. With a resounding thunder of hooves, they assert their dominance, their formidable strength and unyielding resilience rendering even the mightiest of hunters powerless to overcome their ferocious onslaught.

In the vast tapestry of existence, humanity stands akin to the formidable Cape buffalo, navigating the wild currents of life's tumultuous journey. Yet, like the majestic beast, we too find ourselves ensnared at times, ensnared by the tendrils of vice and adversity that threaten to engulf our spirits.

Whether it be the insidious allure of alcoholism, the relentless onslaught of disease, the suffocating grip of poverty, or the protracted trials of lengthy lawsuits, we are all vulnerable to the perils that lurk within the shadows of our own existence. But in the face of such formidable foes, it is imperative that we do not falter, that we do not succumb to the darkness that seeks to claim us.

Instead, we must summon the strength and resilience of the Cape buffalo, rallying our spirits to wage a relentless battle against the forces that seek to ensnare us. With unwavering resolve and unyielding determination, we must fight vigorously to ward off the encroaching shadows, to reclaim our rightful place in the light of hope and possibility.

For it is in the crucible of adversity that the true measure of our humanity is revealed. It is in the face of seemingly insurmountable odds that our spirits are forged, tempered by the fires of adversity and shaped by the crucible of resilience. And though the road may be long and arduous, and the path fraught with obstacles, we must press onward, guided by the indomitable spirit of the Cape buffalo, ever steadfast in our pursuit of triumph over adversity.

5. THE WORLD IS A STAGE, PLAY IT RIGHT

At the highly anticipated annual school day event, the bustling school hall buzzed with excitement as proud parents eagerly awaited the showcase of their children's artistic talents. Among the various performances lined up for the day, a short play featuring elementary school students was a highlight. One of the youngest participants, Little Alan from the first grade, had been assigned a minor role with just a single line of dialogue.

As the curtains drew open and the play commenced, applause filled the air, signaling the commencement of an enchanting display of youthful creativity. Little Alan, clad in his costume, entered the stage punctually at his cue. However, what followed was unexpected; instead of exiting the stage after delivering his lone line, Alan remained stationary, seemingly lost in the moment, gazing at the other characters with wide-eyed innocence.

As seconds stretched into awkward minutes, the audience gradually grasped the unintentional comedy unfolding before them. The play director, realizing the predicament, attempted to discreetly signal Alan to leave the stage, but to no avail. Chuckles and laughter rippled through the crowd as the situation grew increasingly comical.

Recognizing the need to intervene, the play director swiftly made her way onto the stage, gently coaxing Alan to exit the performance area. Despite her best efforts, Alan remained rooted in place, oblivious to the unfolding amusement.

Eventually, with a mixture of patience and gentle guidance, the play director succeeded in leading Alan offstage, restoring order to the performance. Yet, the incident left a lasting impression on the audience, serving as a poignant reminder of the transient nature of life's roles.

The metaphorical concept that "the world is a stage" is deeply resonant, suggesting that life itself is akin to a grand theatrical production, with each individual playing a unique role. In this intricate drama of existence, we are all actors, performing our parts with varying degrees of skill and conviction.

Just as actors in a play must eventually exit the stage once their scene concludes, so too must we gracefully depart from the roles we inhabit throughout our lives. This notion underscores the transient nature of our existence, emphasizing the impermanence of our presence on this vast theatrical landscape.

Staying beyond our allotted time on the stage of life risks transforming us into unwitting jesters, subjects of amusement rather than agents of meaningful contribution. Moreover, lingering past our moment risks intruding upon the narratives of others, usurping roles that rightfully belong to them and disrupting the harmony of the overall production.

Indeed, the wisdom lies in knowing when to make our exit, recognizing the cues that signal the end of our act and gracefully bowing out with dignity and grace. Just as a well-executed departure enhances the overall performance of a play, so too does a timely exit from our roles in life contribute to the coherence and beauty of the human experience.

Ultimately, the maxim "the world is a stage" serves as a poignant reminder of the cyclical nature of life, where beginnings and endings intertwine, and where each individual, in their own time, must take their final curtain call. Embracing this truth allows us to navigate the complexities of existence with humility, authenticity, and a profound appreciation for the roles we play in the grand theater of life.

6. PERIPHERAL VICES

Mrs. Lynn asked her son Tojo for help planting vegetable seedlings. Before they could start planting, Tojo was tasked with removing all the grass from the vegetable garden. Tojo diligently cleared the grass from the garden bed but neglected to remove it from the edges.

When Mrs. Lynn noticed this, she asked Tojo to remove the grass from the edges as well. Tojo replied, "Mom, we are not planting anything on the edge. Let the grass be there."

Weeks later, the vegetable plants thrived, but the garden was soon overrun with grass. The grass that Tojo left on the edges had spread its seeds throughout the garden, eventually outnumbering the vegetable plants.

This situation serves as a metaphor for how seemingly small and peripheral bad behaviors can have a significant impact over time. Habits like smoking, drinking, lying, laziness, and greed may start at the fringes of our lives. However, if not addressed, these behaviors can spread and dominate, affecting our overall success and well-being.

Just as Tojo learned that neglecting the edges of the garden allowed the grass to take over, we must be vigilant in managing our own behaviors. Addressing negative habits early on and maintaining discipline can prevent them from overwhelming our lives and hindering our growth.

7. THE JOURNEY

Alex and his family decided to visit his best friend, who lived in a distant city, after many years. They chose to make the journey by car, anticipating an adventure along the way.

As they drove, they passed through a lush forest, marveling at the sight of blue mountains in the distance crowned by a magnificent waterfall. The road wound through the picturesque countryside, revealing charming villages nestled in the hills. The quaint homes, colorful gardens, and peaceful meadows provided a serene backdrop to their journey.

However, their drive wasn't without its challenges. As they passed through a small city, they encountered rough roads filled with potholes and graffiti-covered walls lining the outskirts. The contrast between the tranquil countryside and the rundown city was stark, yet it added to the tapestry of their journey.

Eventually, the family approached their destination. They crossed a large bridge, which offered a breathtaking view of the sprawling megapolis ahead. The city's skyline, with its towering skyscrapers, signaled the end of their long drive and the beginning of their reunion with Alex's best friend.

This journey is a reflection of life itself. Life is rarely picture perfect. It is filled with ups and downs, moments of beauty and hardship, drama, comedy, tragedy, and adventure. Just like Alex and his family experienced a mix of scenic beauty and urban decay, we too encounter a variety of experiences that shape our journey. Embrace and enjoy each moment, for every experience contributes to the richness of life's adventure.

8. ENVIRONMENT

Pierre decided to plant capsicums (bell pepper) and watermelons in his backyard in mid-spring. He sowed the seeds in pots and placed them in the basement of his house, thinking the seedlings would grow well there. Unfortunately, the basement received only a couple of hours of indirect sunlight each day.

Within a week, the seeds germinated; however, the seedlings were stunted. The humid environment in the basement encouraged fungal growth in the soil, which hindered the plants' development.

Recognizing the problem, Pierre moved the pots outside. Within a couple of days, the plants began to regain their strength and grow healthily. After a week, Pierre transplanted the thriving seedlings into his backyard garden, where they continued to flourish.

This experience illustrates an important principle: individuals are most productive when placed in a supportive environment. Just as Pierre's seedlings struggled in the dark, humid basement, people living in toxic environments are less likely to reach their full potential.

Calm and peaceful homes nurture good citizens. Similarly, schools and universities that emphasize teamwork, laboratory-based projects, creative writing, and free thinking foster creative and knowledgeable students. Workplaces that delegate tasks effectively, grant freedom to work, and instill a sense of purpose will cultivate a highly productive workforce.

A supportive environment, whether in the home, school, or workplace, is crucial for growth and productivity. By ensuring that people are placed in positive settings, we can help them thrive just as Pierre's plants did when given the right conditions.

9. THE RACE

Chris decided to test his new car on a race track, a Bugatti Chiron that was sponsored by a company. He asked his friends to bring their cars to the race track. His friends brought their Porsche, Aston Martin, Koenigsegg, Lamborghini, Ferrari, McLaren, Corvette and Lotus to the race track. Chris' buddy Rick's car was undergoing a major repair; hence he brought his Toyota Corolla to the race track.

The race was scheduled for four hundred miles. At the designated time the race track was "set on fire" by Chris and his friends. The cars zipped fast except one, the Toyota Corolla. The Corolla is not a sports car; it has a top speed of around 140 mph. Rick was an experienced driver; he slammed the accelerator, but the engine would not budge. The engine made a rumbling noise and over heated at the maximum speed. Rick set the speed to 120 mph for the safety of the vehicle.

Chris' Bugatti Chiron broke the 300 mph barrier within a few minutes. All the drivers completed the race within a window of 30 minutes, except Rick's Toyota Corolla.

Upon recruiting a new hire, they are given training on the organizations values, culture and practices. However, there is a limit to training that can be provided to the new recruits. Employees have to align their values with the companies culture and values. Businesses change quickly; for the organization to survive the employees will have to be more creative and bring innovative ideas after the training period. Every employee is responsible for the growth of their organization.

However, some people are untrainable; they will not change their attitude after repeated training. It is not rare to see new recruits burn out after some time if they don't keep up with the companies culture.

10. TRANSFORMATION

Many people assume that motor cars were designed based on horse-drawn carriages. In reality, they were actually modeled after bicycles. Despite the apparent differences between bicycles and cars, the first automobile created by Carl Benz was essentially a modified tricycle. Benz meticulously refined the engine and design over time, eventually leading to the creation of the modern car as we know it today.

Similarly, many founders of major enterprises in the early twentieth century started from humble beginnings. These pioneers often came from rural backgrounds and primarily knew farming. They were largely self-taught, relying on their own ingenuity and persistence. Through numerous failures and learning from their mistakes, they eventually built the large companies that continue to shape our world.

This journey of innovation and growth teaches an important lesson: whatever you build today, no matter how small, has the potential to grow into a large enterprise, creating jobs and opportunities for hundreds of people. The key is to start, be persistent, and continuously learn and improve.

Think of the great inventors and entrepreneurs who began with simple ideas and modest resources. Their success did not come overnight; it was the result of relentless effort, resilience in the face of setbacks, and a commitment to their vision. They started small but thought big, and their contributions transformed industries and lives.

Whether you're an aspiring entrepreneur, an inventor, or someone with a passion project, remember that every large enterprise begins with a single step. Embrace the challenges, learn from your failures, and keep pushing forward. The impact of your efforts might one day be far greater than you ever imagined.

Just start!

11. THE WEIGHT OF POWER

Jameson was a shrewd politician, always with his eyes set on the top seat of the government. He climbed the political ladder through a mix of cunning and unscrupulous tactics, ensuring his ascent by demanding kickbacks on any project he initiated. Praise was a currency he demanded from those around him, using it as a measure of his perceived success and power.

As the leader of his party, Jameson had a penchant for calling country-wide strikes over events occurring in distant lands. He often said to his friends, "You have to put weight and delay things to earn respect from others."

Years passed, and an opportunity arose when the World Development Bank proposed constructing a strategic port to open the economy and create jobs. During the negotiations, a shipping company offered to build the port for free, on the condition that they manage it for a hundred years; in addition the shipping company would pay royalties to the government. However, since Jameson wouldn't receive a cut from this deal, he scuttled the project. Consequently, a neighboring country seized the opportunity, built the port, and prospered as a result.

Eventually, Jameson achieved his ambition and became the president of the country.

Under his rule, no project moved without his "blessings," and the nation was run by his cronies. The populace suffered as inflation soared and poverty increased. Due to misery and unemployment, the youngsters moved to foreign lands to survive.

Several months into his third term, Jameson passed away. Following his wishes, he was cremated. When the crematorium official handed over Jameson's ashes to his son, the son asked, "How much does it weigh?" The official replied, "Three kilograms."

12. THE ERA

Our era is characterized by the time between our birth and our death. During this period, every individual living is a participant in shaping the course of our era and will be evaluated by future generations based on their contributions or lack thereof.

The assessment of an era depends on various factors, including societal, cultural, technological, and environmental aspects. The contributions made by individuals and communities in these areas will play a crucial role in shaping the perception of our era.

One significant aspect of evaluating an era is how well the planet was taken care of during that time. Environmental sustainability and conservation efforts are becoming increasingly critical in the face of climate change, loss of biodiversity, and other ecological challenges. The way we address these issues, such as reducing carbon emissions, protecting natural resources, and promoting sustainable practices, will be key factors in how our era is judged.

Furthermore, the cultural and societal progress made during our time will also influence the evaluation of our era. This includes advancements in human rights, equality, justice, education, healthcare, and overall well-being. It is important to work towards a society that values inclusivity, respects diversity, and ensures the welfare of all its members.

Technological advancements will also be scrutinized when evaluating our era. The development and implementation of innovative technologies that improve people's lives, enhance communication, promote sustainable solutions, and address global challenges will be considered noteworthy contributions.

Collaboration is a key element that drives enterprises forward. Collaboration does not necessarily mean working only with like-minded individuals, but also entails engaging with people who possess different talents, perspectives, and backgrounds. Success in collaboration can be measured by how well you work with those whom you may not naturally gravitate towards or even personally like.

In the context of an era, the same principle applies. The contributions and skills of every person living in that era collectively define its identity and success. By embracing and utilizing the diverse skills and abilities of those around you, you can create a more inclusive and productive environment.

Collaborating with people who have differing opinions, backgrounds, and talents can foster innovation, promote critical thinking, and lead to more comprehensive and well-rounded solutions. It allows for a broader range of ideas, experiences, and expertise to be considered, leading to richer outcomes.

Furthermore, collaborating with those you may not naturally like or agree with challenges your own perspectives and biases. It provides an opportunity for personal growth, empathy, and understanding. Through open dialogue, active listening, and a willingness to find common ground, you can forge productive collaborations and achieve collective goals.

The success of an era is determined by the collective efforts and collaborations of its inhabitants. Embracing the skills and contributions of all individuals, regardless of personal differences, allows for a more comprehensive and impactful era. By working together, leveraging diverse talents, and finding common ground, we can shape a successful and inclusive era that benefits everyone involved.

Ultimately, our era will be evaluated by the future generations. They will analyze our collective actions, achievements, and failures to gauge the impact we had on society, the planet, and the well-being of humanity. It is our responsibility to strive for progress, sustainability, and a better future for generations to come.

13. DEEP CLEANING

After Christopher came home after work he had to mow the lawn as it would be raining continuously for the next five days. The grass had grown thick and tall due to the recent rains.

The grass was not completely dry as two days earlier it was raining. Christopher had only limited time to complete the job as it would be dark in two hours.

It was easy to mow the grass during the initial thirty minutes. However, after some time the engine stalled, though Christopher emptied the lawn mower bag frequently.

Christopher was fed up with the lawn mower after some time. He checked the underside of the lawn mower to see its condition.

When Christopher checked the underside of the lawn mower he saw grass build-up in the deck housing. The gluey grass adhering on the deck housing was so thick that there was hardly any space for the blade to move.

Christopher immediately cleaned the deck housing. He removed all the grass adhering to the deck housing. The lawn mower worked without any glitch once it was cleaned.

While mowing the lawn, Christopher pondered his life. He was very active and had many friends years back. He was promoted several times during the initial phase of his career. However, he had not received a promotion for a long time.

Christopher's early success in his life went to his head. He became arrogant, disrespectful, and hated everyone.

Christopher knew that to progress and move forward, he had to change his attitude and personality. Christopher repented. From that moment he began to treat everyone with respect. A few months later he was promoted.

Christopher was made the head of the training division. Years later he became a member of the companies governing board.

14. MAKING A FOOL OF ONESELF

Miss Kate had recently entered college. As she was far from home she stayed in the student dormitory. One day the students decided to do a party. Miss Kate was assigned to make home made yogurt.

Miss Kate poured equal amount of water to the milk, heated the milk for a few minutes and after it cooled, incubated with the bacterial starter culture.

The following day when Kate checked her bottle of yogurt she was surprised; half the bottle was water, the loose yogurt settled below the water.

Kate poured water into milk thinking that she would get large quantities of yogurt. Kate could not fool the scientific aspect of yogurt making. Kate fooled herself when she added water into milk.

Kate was a brilliant student; however, she was lazy. She was distracted and was not serious in her studies and the grades showed that. The yogurt incident opened here eyes. Kate knew that she was "diluting" her studies by not being serious. Kate took her education seriously after the incident. Today she is a partner in a law firm.

A contractor fools himself when he constructs buildings or roads with inferior quality materials. Similarly, an industrialist cutting corners will see his customers flee. A territory manager fools himself when he meets few clients; at the end of the year he will achieve only a fraction of the target. A politician fools himself when he is corrupt and does not walk the talk. Corruption makes people migrate to distant lands.

15. STANDING OUT AMONGST THE CROWD

Xavier planted his vegetables in a small plot surrounded by a metal fence to prevent the deer and rabbit munching his crop.

One spring season, Xavier planted summer squash and cherry tomatoes. The plants were grown near the edge of the fence. The cherry tomatoes grew well initially; however the large leaves of the summer squash prevented the cherry tomatoes further growth and development, with the exception of one cherry tomato.

When the large leaves of the summer squash prevented the cherry tomato from achieving its objective, it strategized. The cherry tomato grew parallel to the metal fence by clinging to the metal fence. It grew six feet tall producing large number of fruits during its growth.

When new recruits are hired in an organization they are initially given only limited resources. It is up to the new recruit to use his creativity and grow among the seasoned employees of the organization. When new recruits have constraints, they are pushed to find innovative solutions to problems. This kind of thinking can lead to efficient processes and novel approaches that seasoned employees might overlook due to familiarity.

One has to read, attend workshops, collaborate, and execute new ideas continuously thereby improving the growth of the organization. People in the organization notice you when you help the organization grow. This visibility can lead to increased recognition and opportunities for advancement.

16. UNDER PRESSURE

Albin was in a hurry to get to work as he had an important meeting with a client. For breakfast he wished to have string hopper (*idiyappam*). Albin prepared the raw string hopper, placed in the vessel and turned on the stove; he then went for a quick work out.

After the work out, Albin came to have his breakfast. He reached out to the stove to get his breakfast. Unfortunately, Albin forgot to close the vessel; there was no steam build-up to cook the string hopper. Albin closed the vessel; he waited for another 15 minutes to have his breakfast.

Like the string hopper, we perform well under pressure. In fact whatever we are is due to pressure faced throughout our life.

We have been under pressure since we are born. As a child, if we wished to have dessert or candy we had to eat our vegetables and fruits. The good food we ate has significantly impacted our physical and possibly even our emotional well-being.

The exams in school and college days pressured us to study and gain knowledge. The targets and incentives motivate a sales manager to achieve his goals. The publications and patents drive a scientist to perform more and put in grants for research. A hotelier has to excel to attract patrons. The diagnostic chart provided by our physician lead us to change our life-style and behavior.

Being able to excel in high-stress or demanding situations is a valuable skill. Stressful situations can indeed have a profound impact on people's lives. They can push individuals to their limits, forcing them to adapt, grow, and develop resilience. Overcoming adversity can build character, teach valuable life lessons, and help individuals discover their strengths and weaknesses.

17. BREAKING THE VICE

Susan's kitchen was raided by German cockroaches. When Susan complained, her husband Leo purchased some glue boards and kept in the corners of the kitchen. The German cockroaches while roaming around accidentally went into the glue board. They could not move once stuck on to the glue board. They pooped and died on the spot.

We are sometimes trapped in our vice(s). Some of the vices are so powerful that they can ultimately take us down.

The moon has a dark (far) side, a side with densely covered craters. People may also have a dark side that they themselves are ashamed and would like to get rid of.

Once, a young priest from the US was sent to Central America for a meeting. The young priest had poor knowledge of Spanish. While there, the young priest stayed at the local church. It was the Lenten season. The parish priest said in his sermon that they had a guest and introduced the young American priest to the community. The American priest introduced himself in English combined with Spanish. The parish priest stated that the young priest would help him with the confessions later that week.

During the day of the confession, the parish priest only had a few people lined up in front of his confession booth. The parish priest was amazed as usually the whole town would flock to church for confession during the Lenten season.

When the parish priest looked at the other wing of the church he was surprised to see a very long line formed in front of the confession booth managed by the American priest. The people were very happy after the confession. Since the American priest was poor in Spanish, the people confessed all their sins; as he could not understand their language!

In a kitchen, some of the vessels could be cleaned with a sponge; whereas some of the heavily greased vessels require a steel scrubber to clean. Similarly, some of our vices could be easy to get rid of, whereas some may require years of work to be cleaned up.

It may be easy to conquer the whole world, but conquering your vice(s) is extremely challenging. The journey to self improvement is a gradual process and setbacks are common. A purpose driven life, your mission, voluntary work, spirituality, etc., could be helpful in getting rid of your vices.

There is joy in heaven when one person repents than ninety-nine just persons who don't need any repentance (Luke 15:10).

18. THE HEAVENLY BUTTERFLY

Antonio was living on the wrong side of the law. He was notorious in his neighborhood; he would quarrel with neighbors for trivial reasons. His greed for money ended up working for the mafia.

Antonio's family was sad seeing his behavior. No matter how hard they pleaded, Antonio never quit his evil ways.

One day while quarreling with a rival, Antonio was badly hurt. He was taken to the hospital. Seeing the agony and sadness of his family and reflecting his life, Antonio repented. A couple of days later Antonio died.

When Antonio reached the heavenly gate, St. Peter greeted him.

St. Peter opened a big book and went through the not-so-fabulous life of Antonio. St. Peter said, "Hmmm...God wish to see you. You will see him in a few moments."

Moments later Antonio was in front of God. Antonio was nervous; he knew his eternal life would be in trouble if he would not act promptly.

When Antonio was in front of God, he saw his entire life in front of him. God asked, "Give me a reason why you should live here?"

Antonio replied, "God, do you like butterflies?"

God stated, "Of course I do. See my majestic garden; it has plenty of butterflies."

Antonio saw that the garden of paradise had thousands of different types of butterflies.

Antonio said, "I hope you know the life cycle of butterflies. My life can be compared to the life cycle of a butterfly. My life on Earth can be compared to a caterpillar."

Antonio continued, "My death is the cocoon stage of a butterfly. My body is still in the casket, in the grave. Currently, I am in the butterfly stage, marveled by God himself."

God couldn't stop laughing. He stated majestically, "You floored me."

When St. Peter glanced, he saw God walking with Antonio in the garden.

19. THE BROKER

Stan and Ted were neighbors in a city. Though they were wealthy, Stan was humble and a voracious reader. Once Stan and Ted met Patrick, a real estate broker at a meeting. Patrick was very hard working and knew the "pulse" of the city. As he was a good in his trade, he knew most important people in the city.

One day Patrick went to Ted's house and stated about a large marsh land available for sale. Patrick stated that the owner need money for an emergency and may be negotiable. Ted laughed at him.

Patrick went to Stan's house and repeated the information. Stan said, "I am sure the city will be run out of land in a few years and will have to expand. The marsh land will have value then."

Stan continued, " I like the proposal, but I don't have ready money to buy it."

Patrick stated, "That is not a problem, I know a banker that can help you. He offers very low interest loans. Moreover we can negotiate with the seller and reduce the asking price."

Stan and Patrick worked together, negotiated the price and quickly purchased the marsh land within a couple of weeks.

A few years later commercial contractors approached Stan for the marsh land. Stan developed the property and sold it at a good price.

Stan and Patrick collaborated on several business ventures.

A few years later, Patrick passed away. When Ted wanted to improve his business, he searched for Patrick. Ted was sad to hear the demise of Patrick.

Years later, Stan was the wealthiest man in the city. Ted was in awe of his neighbor's wealth.

In your life, there may be several people that may offer their assistance and support, and it's important to recognize and appreciate their contributions to your life. The people who try to help you can be your parents, siblings, relatives, friends, or anyone with a face. Life is finite, and none of us know how much time we have. It is essential to cherish the moments and relationships we have because they may not last forever. Gratitude can strengthen relationships and create a sense of reciprocity. Making well-informed and thoughtful choices is crucial because decisions can have long-lasting consequences. Being diligent and considering the potential outcomes of your choices is a valuable skill. While the people you interact with today may not be around tomorrow, it's important to plan and make decisions that can positively impact your future.

The next generation may not be concerned with your priorities, wealth and happiness.

20. FINANCIAL DISCIPLINE

Margaret worked at a lawyer's office working as a secretary for Aaron a respected lawyer. Margaret always asked for a raise. Aaron tried to help her as much as he could.

Aaron closely observed the behavior of Margaret. One day, when Margaret raised the issue of a salary hike, Aaron asked her to come to his office.

When Margaret sat down, Aaron took a piece of paper. Aaron asked Margaret, "I see you have coffee from the coffee shop daily. How much do you pay for your coffee?

Margaret replied, "I pay $4.00 for coffee."

Aaron did his calculation. "There are around 20 working days per month. $4X20 days = $80 per month. That is $80X12 months = $960.00 per year for coffee alone." "I am not including the tip you pay."

Aaron continued, "I see you having lunch from the cafeteria. How much do you 7.00 per day."

Aaron did his calculation. He stated," The cafeteria lunch comes to $1680.00 per year."

Aaron asked how much she pays for bottled water every month. Margaret replied, "At least $20 per month."

Aaron did his calculations, "That is a cool $240.00 per year."

"I see you driving a high-end SUV, I am sure you are leasing the vehicle and you pay at least $600.00 every month."

Margaret nodded, "Yes, you are right."

Aaron stated, "The lease comes to $7200.00 per year. I bet you pay good money as insurance premium, in addition to the service charges for maintaining this high-end vehicle."

Aaron did the final calculations. 960+1680+240+7200 = $10,080.00

Aaron showed the figures to Margaret. "You are throwing $10,080.00 every year. "This is huge money, based on your salary," remarked Aaron.

Aaron continued, "If you make your own coffee in the office using instant coffee, use the filtered water from our office, bring your own lunch, and go for an ordinary car, you save a ton of money. If you look carefully, I am sure you will find there may be several other activities that you could rid off."

Margaret went home and thought about Aaron's suggestions.

She understood that she could get rid off many behaviors and activities that cost her plenty of money.

Eventually, Margaret enrolled in an evening class. She earned a degree in Finance and Investment. She became a financial consultant and currently advice large companies.

21. THE SHIRT

Ralph is a senior executive at a company. He wears expensive 'Dior" shirts to his office meetings. He takes great care of his expensive shirts. He washes and irons it carefully. People always admired Ralphs dressing. Years later, when the shirt lost its sheen, he donated the shirt to the Salvation Army.

However, when Ralph is home he wears cheaper shirts. He wears those shirts when he paints the house, does the gardening or washes his car. Ralph's house wear shirts have stains from painting and gardening. Years later, when the shirt was no longer wearable, he used it as a mop for cleaning his garage.

Similar is the situation for people. If you burn the midnight oil, study hard, you will be given a good position based on your qualifications. You will have a value in society. When you retire, you have a choice to move to any place, play golf, travel the world and enjoy the good life.

When you are in school, if you waste your time without regard for studies, with time you will be working for someone who will not value you. You will be working for employers who will be abusing you; you will be working with minimum pay for extended period of time. Retirement will be a dream that you cannot afford.

Use your time judiciously. When you look back after sometime do not regret.

22. PRIORITY

The priorities of man changes with time. For a toddler a piece of paper, plastic or a feather is enough to make him happy. Several years later, playing with a plastic toy may be his priority. At age 8-10, having good food, possessing a cycle or a sports ball and bat is his priority.

Once a child is into his teenage years, watching movies, sports and video games may be his priority. At the end of the teenage years having a motorbike or car may be his priority. He also dreams to get into the best university. A job at a multinational company may be the priority in the early 20s. Finding a spouse is the priority in the late 20s or early 30s. Climbing the executive ladder and buying a house may be the priority in the mid 30s. Having a six or seven figure salary may be the priority in the forties. Changing the small house to a larger one is another priority. Reaching the apex of the organization is his dream in the fifties.

Maintaining health and touring the world may be the priority in the sixties and early seventies. Transferring to a small house or old age home may be the priority in the late seventies. By the eighties, the body may turn to be a prison. At that age, the body and mind may not be in sync. People wish to leave the body for the eternal world.

23. MAINTAIN A SHARP BRAIN THROUGHOUT LIFE

Maintaining a sharp brain until death is essential for a fulfilling and independent life. Cognitive health plays a crucial role in overall well-being, influencing everything from daily functioning to emotional stability. As we age, preserving mental acuity becomes increasingly important for several reasons:

A sharp mind enables you to engage fully with the world around you. It allows for continued learning, problem-solving, and participation in a wide range of activities. This engagement not only enriches your life but also brings joy and satisfaction as you navigate various experiences and challenges.

Cognitive health is critical for maintaining independence. Tasks such as managing finances, remembering important dates, and making informed decisions require mental sharpness. By keeping your brain active and healthy, you can sustain your ability to live independently and avoid reliance on others for basic daily functions.

Mental acuity is closely linked to emotional health. A sharp brain helps regulate emotions, cope with stress, and maintain a positive outlook. Cognitive decline can lead to frustration, anxiety, and depression, but staying mentally active and engaged can mitigate these effects and promote emotional resilience.

Cognitive health fosters strong social connections. Engaging in conversations, remembering names and events, and participating in social activities are easier when your mind is sharp. These connections are vital for emotional support, reducing feelings of loneliness, and enhancing overall happiness.

There is a significant interplay between cognitive health and physical well-being. A sharp mind contributes to better physical health by enabling you to adhere to healthy habits, follow medical advice, and engage in regular physical activity.

Proactively maintaining brain health can help protect against cognitive decline and neurodegenerative diseases such as Alzheimer's and dementia. Activities that challenge the brain, such as puzzles, reading, and learning new skills, can strengthen neural connections and promote brain plasticity.

By prioritizing cognitive health and adopting a proactive approach, you can maintain a sharp brain throughout your life. This not only enhances your quality of life but also ensures you remain active, independent, and engaged in the world around you, fostering a sense of purpose and fulfillment until the very end.

24. ADAPTABILITY

It is not the strongest nor the most intelligent of species that survives, it is the one that is most adaptable to change. - *Charles Darwin*

Physical or mental strength can be advantageous in certain situations. It might provide a competitive edge, especially in environments where raw power is crucial. Over-reliance on strength alone can be limiting, as it may not be suitable for all challenges or changing circumstances. Strength can become a liability if the environment requires flexibility and quick adaptation.

Intelligence allows for problem-solving, strategic thinking, and the ability to navigate complex situations. It can be a valuable asset in a wide range of scenarios. High intelligence does not guarantee adaptability. In fact, highly intelligent individuals may face challenges if they are resistant to change or unable to apply their intelligence in dynamic, evolving situations.

Adaptability is the ability to adjust and thrive in changing circumstances. It allows individuals or species to respond effectively to new challenges, opportunities, or threats. Adaptability involves the ability to adjust to new conditions, environments, or situations. It involves being open to change, learning from experiences, and evolving strategies as needed.

Adaptability also involves the willingness to embrace and adjust one's approach. The world is moving quickly, one should be receptive to new ideas, perspectives, and ways of doing things. Adaptable people continuously acquire new skills and knowledge to stay relevant. They find creative solutions in unfamiliar or unpredictable situations. In the workplace, adaptable individuals contribute to innovation and problem-solving. In personal life, adaptability fosters resilience in the face of life's uncertainties.

Adaptability is a key attribute in the work culture of successful organizations. An adaptable work culture is one that embraces change, encourages innovation, and empowers employees to navigate evolving circumstances.

Open and transparent communication is vital for an adaptable work culture. Leaders should keep employees informed about changes, the reasons behind them, and how they fit into the organization's overall strategy.

An adaptable culture involves agile decision-making processes. Teams should be empowered to make decisions quickly and efficiently, allowing the organization to respond promptly to challenges and opportunities.

Diversity in the workforce contributes to adaptability. A diverse range of perspectives and experiences helps the organization approach problems from multiple angles and fosters creative solutions.

Regular feedback loops and opportunities for reflection contribute to an adaptable work culture. Employees should feel comfortable sharing feedback and insights, helping the organization learn and improve over time.

Building resilience among employees is part of an adaptable work culture. This involves acknowledging challenges, learning from setbacks, and focusing on solutions rather than dwelling on problems.

Organizations with an adaptable work culture are better positioned to navigate uncertainties, capitalize on opportunities, and maintain a competitive edge in the fast-paced business environment. Such cultures foster a sense of agility and innovation, making employees more engaged, motivated, and committed to the organization's success.

25. DYSBIOTIC POPULACE

Dysbiosis (Greek, bad way of living) is the imbalance in the microbial community within the body. It is often associated with changes in diet or due to inappropriate use of antibiotics. Abuse of antibiotics could prop up harmful bacteria like *Clostridioides difficile* that causes diarrhea and damage to the colon if not treated properly.

A country is as good as the people inhabiting it. It is the quality of the people that determines the quality of the country. A "dysbiotic populace" is detrimental to the country. In a democracy everyone has the right to elect capable administrators. If the policies of the administrators are ineffective, citizens often contemplate moving to distant lands.

Patriotism, being a transient sentiment, can wane under the pressures of various forms of hunger, both physical and intellectual, prompting individuals to seek opportunities elsewhere. In a democracy, it becomes the duty of the populace to discern and choose the most qualified candidates. The absence of visionary individuals can lead to an exodus of talent. Once talented individuals depart, the vacuum is filled by less desirable "vipers and bears."

A government, no matter its structure, cannot effectively govern in the absence of talented individuals. Current examples such as Haiti and Somalia stand as classical illustrations of nations grappling with a deficiency in effective governance.

Over time, philosophical perspectives evolve, making it challenging to ascertain the true intentions of elected officials. Entrusting governance without reservations, assuming virtuous intentions, is not a prudent approach. Citizens should have the power to remove elected officials from office before their term is complete if they are dissatisfied with their performance or if there are concerns about their actions. To ensure effective administration, there should be the right to recall every two years, providing a mechanism for accountability. Right to recall highlights the importance of an engaged and vigilant citizenry in the democratic process. This perspective aligns with the idea that democracy requires active participation and oversight by the people to function optimally. The underlying goal is to promote effective administration, emphasizing that governance should not only be about good intentions but also about delivering results and meeting the needs of the people.

26. THE RUBIK'S CUBE

The Rubik's cube holds widespread appeal as a beloved toy among the younger generation. Mastering the solution to the Rubik's cube requires the memorization of numerous algorithms, coupled with deft manipulation of its layers in a matter of seconds. It is not unusual to witness enthusiastic young individuals completing the algorithm in less than five seconds, while others may perceive the process as an insurmountable challenge.

This analogy seamlessly extends into the domain of administrators. When a new administrator joins a company or is tasked with managing a tumultuous situation, the range of responses is notably diverse. Some administrators grapple with the intricacies, finding it challenging to formulate effective solutions, while others exhibit remarkable adeptness in navigating the complexities of their responsibilities.

The parallels between administrators and Rubik's cube solving become even more evident when considering the contrasting approaches adopted by individuals in these roles. Analogous to enthusiasts swiftly deciphering the Rubik's cube algorithm, certain administrators demonstrate proficiency in efficiently navigating challenges. These adept administrators not only find resolutions but do so with an efficiency that positively impacts the lives of employees or citizens involved.

Fundamentally, administrators' proficiency in troubleshooting and streamlining processes emerges as a defining factor in their success. Those who encounter difficulties may struggle to grasp the intricate workings of the organizational landscape or the complexities inherent in the challenges they face. In contrast, administrators who excel possess a keen ability to decode complexities, implementing solutions that not only address immediate concerns but also contribute to the overall enhancement of operational efficiency.

The analogy transcends mere problem-solving, encapsulating the adaptability, resilience, and strategic thinking exhibited by administrators—attributes honed by Rubik's cube enthusiasts. As administrators navigate the dynamic landscape of their responsibilities, the diversity in outcomes mirrors the varying results observed in the art of Rubik's cube solving. Some maneuver with finesse, while others grapple with intricacies. In this analogy, both realms underscore the significance of skill, experience, and the ability to swiftly decipher and address challenges for ultimate success. Ultimately, achieving success in both scenarios relies on the capacity to apply knowledge and strategies in an ever-evolving environment. Top-notch administrators, akin to adept Rubik's cube solvers, integrate expertise, adaptability, and sound decision-making to effectively navigate the challenges presented before them.

27. WORTH OF A DIAMOND

The worth of a diamond increases with time. A diamond mined a century ago commands a significant higher price in the current market. Just like a diamond's value can appreciate over the years due to various factors, an individual's value in the professional arena can increase with time through a combination of education, experience, and continuous learning.

Think of education as the initial mining process for a diamond. It provides the foundation for an individual, shaping their basic attributes, knowledge, and skills. Completing formal education is comparable to unearthing a raw diamond from the earth. It is valuable, but its true worth becomes apparent after it undergoes the refinement process.

Professional and volunteering experiences can be likened to the cutting, polishing, and shaping of a raw diamond. These experiences refine an individual's skills, allowing them to shine in their chosen field. The challenges faced and lessons learned during work and volunteer opportunities contribute to the development of expertise and a well-rounded skill set.

Continuing education acts as ongoing maintenance for the diamond. Just as a diamond may be re-cut to enhance its brilliance, individuals can pursue further education to stay current in their field and adapt to changing trends. Whether through workshops, certifications, or advanced degrees, continuing education ensures that an individual's knowledge remains sharp and relevant.

Like a well-cut diamond that reflects light from multiple facets, an individual with diverse experiences and a commitment to learning becomes adaptable and versatile. The ability to apply knowledge across various situations and industries makes an individual more valuable in a dynamic and ever-changing professional landscape.

As the refined diamond becomes more valuable over time, an individual's professional value increases with each experience, accomplishment, and learning opportunity. The cumulative effect of education, experience, and ongoing learning positions an individual as an asset, sought after in their field.

28. LABOR OF LOVE

After dedicating many years of service, Tam retired from her role as Chief Financial Officer. During her farewell event, she shared excerpts from her memoir.

Tam's journey began during the height of the Vietnam civil war when she and her family had to flee, boarding a boat with their belongings. Unfortunately, they were attacked by pirates, losing everything except the clothes on their backs. After months at sea, they eventually landed in a distant land before finally settling in the United States.

Initially taking a farm job where she earned a modest income, Tam's life took a positive turn when she received a significant amount of $20.00 one day!

Determined to build a better future, Tam later secured a position as a glass-washing aide at a university. Her initial aspiration was to pursue a career in the clinical laboratory, but life had other plans. She found herself gravitating towards the accounting department of the university, where she discovered a true passion for numbers and finance. She excelled in her roles, eventually managing grants with great proficiency.

Tam's dedication to her education did not waver. She pursued a management course in the evenings and, within a few years, proudly earned her MBA with a specialization in Finance. Her hard work and expertise did not go unnoticed. When the CFO of the institute retired, Tam was promoted to fill the role. Known for her exceptional work ethic, she responded to emails within twenty minutes, even in the middle of the night. Over the years, she trained scores of people, many of whom went on to secure highly paying jobs at various universities.

Outside of work, Tam enjoyed playing golf with her husband on weekends. She was also known for her culinary skills, cooking for all the staff during the institute's annual food festival.

At the age of 65, Tam decided it was time to retire and spend more time with her grandchildren. Before settling into her new life, she planned to tour the world, starting with a visit to her birthplace in Vietnam. Her journey was a testament to resilience, hard work, and the pursuit of dreams against all odds.

When people work with their heart, their dedication and passion shine through in their efforts. However, Tam's successors, despite enjoying a comfortable life, struggled to command the same level of respect. Their secure and easy lifestyle, while beneficial in many ways, seemed to dilute the fervor and drive that often earn admiration and reverence in the workplace.

The lack of hardships or challenges that Tam's successors faced may have contributed to a perception of complacency or lack of genuine commitment. Unlike those who pour their heart into their work, often driven by passion and a sense of purpose, Tam's successors may have lacked the same intensity and zeal. This disparity in dedication became apparent in their work ethic, making it difficult for them to inspire and garner respect from their peers and subordinates.

True respect in a professional setting often stems from witnessing someone's relentless effort, resilience, and heartfelt dedication. While comfort and ease in life are desirable, they can sometimes lead to a disconnect from the values of hard work and perseverance that inspire others. Thus, Tam's successors, though living comfortably, missed out on the profound respect that comes from working with one's heart and soul, fully invested in their craft.

29. THE MOST VALUABLE TIME

Embarking on a journey via airplane is undoubtedly an exhilarating experience. The thrill of soaring through the skies and witnessing breathtaking landscapes from above adds an element of joy to the adventure. However, amidst the excitement, it is essential to acknowledge the uncertainties that come with air travel.

While the idea of not reaching your destination may seem disconcerting, it is important to recognize that airports serve as secure havens. The stringent regulations, advanced security measures, and cutting-edge technologies implemented in air travel collectively contribute to making airplanes one of the safest modes of transportation.

Despite the reassurance provided by aviation safety protocols, it is crucial to be prepared for unexpected situations. In the event of an emergency, passengers are required to evacuate the aircraft within a remarkably short timeframe—just 90 seconds. This rapid evacuation mandate applies universally, irrespective of the size of the commercial airliner.

During such scenarios, passengers are explicitly instructed not to retrieve their carry-on bags. Any delay in complying with this directive can potentially jeopardize the safety of all on board. Therefore, understanding the gravity of the situation and acting swiftly is paramount.

Given these circumstances, it becomes imperative to consider what essentials to carry in your pockets while flying. Naturally, there's a limit to the number of items you can stow, necessitating a focus on the most critical belongings. These include your identification cards, credit cards, house and car keys, and, of course, your cell phone—a lifeline in many situations.

For those engaged in business or requiring secure data, an external USB drive proves invaluable. If you have presentations or sensitive information to discuss with clients, ensuring that these files are stored on an external drive allows for easy accessibility and safeguarding of crucial data.

Additionally, if you happen to wear a coat, utilizing its pockets strategically can enhance your preparedness. Placing your passport securely in a coat pocket, for instance, ensures that this vital document remains easily accessible throughout your journey. Ensure that you keep your belongings organized as they may become disarrayed after passing through airport security.

In essence, while the thrill of flying is undeniable, a thoughtful consideration of safety measures and preparedness ensures that every traveler can navigate the skies with confidence and peace of mind.

30. THE CONTAINER

The constant presence of trucks transporting containers on our roads is a testament to the intricate dance of global commerce. These containers, resembling massive metal giants, cradle within them a vast spectrum of goods that mirrors the diversity of human needs and desires. From the freshness of fruits and fish to the technological marvels of electronic goods, the sturdiness of furniture, the simplicity of paper, the intricacy of automobile parts, and the joy of sports goods – the contents of these containers encapsulate the essence of a thriving, interconnected world.

Behind the steel walls of each container lies more than just products; they encapsulate the collective efforts and aspirations of hundreds of employees. These workers, dispersed across the globe, contribute their skills, labor, and creativity to manufacture and assemble the myriad items that find their way into these moving warehouses on wheels. A container filled with fruits is a testament to the dedication of farmers, pickers, and packers. Electronic goods embody the collective ingenuity of engineers, assembly line workers, and designers. Furniture and automobile parts carry the marks of craftsmanship from carpenters, welders, and technicians. The variety is as extensive as the range of goods transported.

These containers, often seen as mere vessels for transporting products, play a vital role in the economic vitality of a country. The goods they carry are not just commodities; they represent the lifeblood of industries, the backbone of economies, and the source of revenue that sustains nations. The activity surrounding these containers fuels trade, creates job opportunities, and stimulates economic growth.

Moreover, the impact of these containers extends beyond economic considerations. They are integral to the daily lives of people, providing the goods that make modern life possible. From the essentials of food and shelter to the conveniences of technology and entertainment, these containers bring forth the products that shape our existence.

In essence, the sight of trucks hauling containers on the road is more than a mundane spectacle; it is a visual manifestation of the interconnected and interdependent world we inhabit. Each container is a microcosm of global collaboration, where the labor of countless individuals converges to create the vast tapestry of goods that enrich our lives and drive the wheels of progress.

31. THE RACE TRACK

Jobin, a high-ranking executive at a Fortune 500 company, boasts an impressive educational background from prestigious colleges and universities. Despite being provided a life of privilege, his journey has been marred by a lack of judicious decision-making. His character flaws are apparent – an arrogance that breeds disdain for those who outshine him intellectually and a deep-seated detestation for the underprivileged.

An interesting turn of events unfolds when a client extends an invitation to Jobin, inviting him to a race track. The track, devoid of the usual hustle and bustle due to being off-season, becomes the setting for an unconventional experience. The client, seeking to inject an element of thrill, suggests they hop into a two-seater Formula One car. However, despite the empty and secure environment of the race track, Jobin surprises everyone by driving at an unusually slow pace, a manifestation of his underlying fear.

The experience at the race track serves as a catalyst for Jobin's introspection that night. Despite his stellar educational background and the privilege he has enjoyed, he realizes that his life lacks a meaningful and purposeful direction. The revelation strikes him: though surrounded by brilliant minds during his academic years, he never reached out for collaboration. In his professional journey, he never harnessed his intellect and creativity to contribute meaningfully to the company. Instead, he opted for the bare minimum, resulting in the stunted growth of his department.

Jobin's contemplation unveils the broader pattern of missed opportunities and untapped potential. The realization that he harbors an aversion to collaboration and innovation dawns upon him. His reluctance to engage with those brighter than him and his disdain for the underprivileged have shaped a career marked by mediocrity.

As dawn breaks, Jobin is faced with a choice – to continue down the path of stagnation or to embrace change, collaboration, and creativity. The race track experience becomes a metaphor for his life, prompting him to reevaluate his priorities and embark on a journey of personal and professional growth. The echoes of his ponderings resonate, challenging him to break free from the constraints of fear and arrogance that have hindered his true potential.

32. ONE KEY PIANO

The piano, an intricate musical instrument, comprises a set of keys spanning seven octaves, with each octave consisting of 12 notes, encompassing both sharps and flats. Playing these keys in a skillful and artistic manner gives rise to a harmonious melody that captivates the listener.

Within certain organizational structures, a dynamic unfolds where some executive leaders exhibit a preference for specific individuals or divisions over others. This preferential treatment can manifest as unequal opportunities, recognition, or resources. Unfortunately, this biased approach often results in a disparity where some hardworking individuals find themselves receiving less acknowledgment and support.

Despite the dedication and effort exerted by certain teams or individuals, they may encounter a seemingly unfair distribution of attention and resources, akin to a step-motherly attitude. This disparity can lead to demotivation among those who feel overlooked or undervalued. Consequently, these once-productive teams may either disengage, seek opportunities elsewhere, or succumb to a decline in morale.

Drawing a parallel to the musical analogy of a piano, an effective leader can be likened to a skilled piano player. A successful leader possesses the ability to discern the nuances of the organizational "keys" and understands when and how to play them strategically. Just as a piano player crafts a beautiful composition by skillfully navigating the keys, a successful leader orchestrates a harmonious workplace by recognizing and valuing the diverse talents and efforts within the organization. In doing so, they contribute to the sustained motivation and success of the entire team, preventing the gradual withering of the organizational fabric.

33. REMEBERING YOU

The concept that, after two to three generations following our demise, the collective memory of our existence fades away is rooted in the acknowledgment of the ephemeral nature of individual remembrance within the broader scope of history. It reflects the understanding that, over time, personal stories and experiences tend to dissipate as subsequent generations emerge with their own narratives and concerns.

This phenomenon is influenced by various factors. Firstly, the passage of time inherently results in the dilution of personal connections and memories. As new generations arise, their focus naturally shifts towards contemporary issues and experiences, relegating the details of past individuals to the periphery of collective consciousness.

Moreover, societal and cultural changes play a pivotal role. As norms, values, and perspectives evolve, the relevance of the stories of past generations may diminish, making it more challenging for individuals to maintain a connection with the lives and experiences of their ancestors.

Technological advancements and the globalization of information also contribute to this process. The vast amount of information available in the digital age can lead to a saturation of historical narratives, making it difficult for individual stories to endure beyond a certain timeframe. Additionally, the interconnectedness of the world means that people may be more attuned to global events and contemporary issues than the specific details of their familial or ancestral past.

Despite these considerations, the impact of an individual's existence can endure in more indirect ways, such as through cultural or familial traditions, genetic legacies, or tangible contributions to society that leave a lasting imprint. While personal memories may fade, the influence of past generations can persist in the broader context of the legacies they leave behind.

In essence, the understanding that individual remembrance tends to wane after a few generations serves as a contemplative observation on the transient nature of personal legacies in the grand tapestry of human history. It underscores the importance of cherishing moments, making meaningful contributions, and understanding the evolving nature of memory in the continuum of time.

34. THE POWERLESS GOD

The concept that God can accomplish anything in the world is a prevailing belief among believers. In Matthew 13:58, it is mentioned that Jesus could not perform miracles in a particular place due to the people's lack of belief. This highlights the significance of faith in the divine ability to manifest miracles. The verse suggests that God's actions are often contingent upon the faith of individuals. Without faith, the connection between humanity and the divine may be hindered, limiting the manifestation of divine miracles.

Faith is not merely a passive acknowledgment of God's abilities; rather, it is portrayed as an active and dynamic force that propels the divine to interact with the human realm. The emphasis on faith as a pivotal factor underscores the idea that the connection between humanity and the divine is a reciprocal and participatory relationship. It implies that faith acts as a conduit through which divine energy flows into the lives of individuals and communities.

In the absence of faith, this connection becomes strained and may even be hindered. The limitations on the manifestation of divine miracles are intricately tied to the openness and receptivity of individuals. It suggests that faith is not only a personal conviction but also a catalyst that unlocks the full potential of divine intervention. Without this essential element, the transformative power of God's miracles may remain dormant, waiting to be activated by the genuine and unwavering faith of believers.

This perspective encourages believers to nurture and deepen their faith, recognizing it as a dynamic force that shapes their spiritual journey. It prompts introspection and underscores the significance of an active, trusting relationship with the divine. The intertwining of faith and divine intervention, as emphasized by this belief, invites individuals to actively engage in their spirituality, fostering a connection that goes beyond mere acknowledgment to a profound and transformative experience of the divine in their lives.

A poignant representation of this concept can be found in the widely traveled painting titled "The Light of the World" by English artist William Holman Hunt. The painting depicts Jesus knocking on a door, and notably, the door lacks a latch. This absence of a latch symbolizes that the decision to allow God into one's life rests entirely with the individual on the other side of the door. It underscores the personal responsibility of opening oneself to the divine and inviting spiritual transformation through faith.

For individuals who hold faith in God, their spiritual beliefs often serve as a moral compass, guiding them towards acts of kindness and service to others. The teachings of various religious texts often encourage followers to love their neighbors, show mercy, and contribute to the welfare of the community.

35. PARTY TO A CRIME

Arthur embarked on a journey to visit his friend in the bustling city. As he strolled through the neighborhood, he couldn't help but notice its less-than-perfect ambiance. Despite the surroundings, Arthur enjoyed a pleasant hour chatting with his friend. However, upon returning to his car, he was met with a disheartening sight – someone had maliciously used a metal object to scratch the paint on both sides of his vehicle. A wave of horror washed over Arthur, leaving him dismayed. His friend empathetically expressed sorrow for the unfortunate incident.

In the broader context of societal dynamics, when an individual with genuine intentions to contribute to social service steps forward, it is not uncommon to encounter disparaging remarks from dishonest individuals. These negative comments create a ripple effect, discouraging the sincere person and potentially driving them away from their altruistic endeavors. Unfortunately, this societal response inadvertently supports incompetence, as the honest individual may be deterred from pursuing their noble cause.

Moreover, the dishonest individuals, fueled by corrupt motives, often manage to seize positions that should rightfully be occupied by those with integrity. This distortion in the allocation of roles and responsibilities perpetuates a cycle where the undeserving hold sway, while the deserving are sidelined by the unwarranted influence of dishonesty.

Certain underdeveloped countries find themselves perpetually stuck in a state of stagnation, maintaining the status quo. This persistent condition can be attributed to the influence of corrupt administrators and their cohorts, who actively thwart the entry of honest individuals into positions of authority. The entrenched system is designed to resist positive change and development, serving the interests of a select few rather than the collective welfare of the nation.

The corrupt administrators, forming a close-knit coterie, create a barrier against the influx of individuals with genuine intentions to bring about positive transformations. Honest and capable individuals often find themselves excluded from key decision-making roles, hindering the country's progress and perpetuating a cycle of underdevelopment.

Furthermore, the complicity of the general population in this situation cannot be overlooked. Some members of society may be inadvertently contributing to the maintenance of the status quo through either passive acceptance or direct involvement in corrupt practices. This collaboration, whether intentional or coerced, reinforces the grip of corruption on the nation, making it challenging for any sincere efforts to break through and instigate meaningful change.

In essence, the entwined dynamics of corrupt leadership and the complicity of the populace collectively contribute to the persistent underdevelopment experienced by certain countries, creating a formidable challenge for those seeking to usher in positive reforms.

36. SHADOW OF DEATH

Our existence on Earth is bound by the constraints of finite time. The ominous presence of death casts a perpetual shadow over our lives. Its looming specter, an ever-present reminder of our mortality, influences the way we perceive and navigate our existence. The shadow of death, a silent companion from the moment we take our first breath, serves as a poignant reflection on the transient nature of life. In recognizing this inescapable reality, we are prompted to contemplate the significance of our time on this planet and the legacy we aim to leave behind. The shadow, though daunting, can also be a catalyst for introspection, motivating us to live purposefully, cherish moments, and contribute meaningfully to the world around us. Thus, as we navigate the complex tapestry of life, the shadow of death becomes a compelling force urging us to embrace the richness of our journey with mindfulness and purpose.

At the inception of our existence, we entered this world devoid of possessions or preconceived notions. Stripped of material wealth, our journey through life becomes a canvas upon which our actions are painted. It is the choices we make, whether benevolent or malevolent, that shape the narrative of our legacy. Unlike material possessions, our deeds are indelible imprints that persist beyond the temporal confines of our earthly sojourn.

Our legacy is not an external bequest but an internal resonance of the impact we have on the world. Every act, be it virtuous or otherwise, becomes a thread in the tapestry of our life story. It is a testament to our character, reflecting the essence of who we are and the mark we leave on the collective memory of those we encounter.

As we traverse the intricate path of existence, the echoes of our actions reverberate through time, creating a ripple effect that extends far beyond the boundaries of our immediate experience. Therefore, the realization that our legacy is a product of our choices underscores the profound responsibility we bear in crafting a narrative that transcends the limitations of our temporal existence. In essence, the legacy we bequeath is not merely a reflection of our past but a compass guiding the future perceptions of those who follow in our footsteps.

37. OVERCOMING CHALLENGES

Adolfo is responsible for getting his children to school by 8:15 AM, and any lateness would result in a "tardy" mark on their report cards. One morning, they encountered a roadblock due to a fallen tree while on their way to school. Fortunately, Adolfo was familiar with the nearby lanes, so he reversed his car and navigated through them, ensuring they reached the school on time.

Being in an executive role entail facing a diverse range of challenges, and it is a reality that not every day unfolds seamlessly. The professional landscape is dynamic, and executives frequently encounter hurdles in their path. These obstacles can take various forms, such as market fluctuations, unexpected crises, or internal organizational complexities.

Executives are entrusted with leadership positions precisely because they possess the acumen to navigate such challenges. Their role goes beyond managing day-to-day operations; it involves strategic thinking, decision-making, and the ability to adapt swiftly to changing circumstances. In essence, executives are not only responsible for the success of their departments or organizations but also for steering through uncertainties and ensuring sustained progress.

The capacity to figure out the next best step is a hallmark of effective leadership. Executives must analyze situations, weigh options, and make informed decisions that align with the overarching goals of the organization. This skill set goes hand in hand with the strategic vision that executives are expected to bring to the table.

Furthermore, the leadership role demands resilience and the ability to inspire confidence among team members during challenging times. Executives often serve as role models, setting the tone for how the organization responds to adversity. Their strategic thinking and decisiveness contribute not only to overcoming obstacles but also to fostering a culture of adaptability and continuous improvement within the organization.

38. RETIREMENT

After a dedicated career spanning 35 years, Bernard chose to retire from his role as an educator. Throughout his tenure, he exhibited a relentless commitment to personal growth, making it a daily practice to expand his own knowledge. Bernard's teaching methodology was characterized by a forward-thinking approach, ensuring that he imparted cutting-edge concepts to his students.

In a classroom, students hail from diverse societal backgrounds. Over time, Bernard has assisted students requiring financial support, ensuring they not only receive aid but also helping them secure part-time jobs, including teaching assistant positions, to empower them to stand independently.

His impact on the lives of his students was truly remarkable. A significant number of them emerged as influential figures in society, with many transitioning into successful entrepreneurs. Collectively, the ventures initiated by his former students now generate an impressive revenue of approximately $200 billion. Bernard's legacy extends beyond the confines of the classroom, shaping the trajectory of his students' careers and contributing significantly to the socioeconomic landscape.

Retirement marks a pivotal phase in one's life, providing an opportunity for introspection and reflection. Within this diverse group of retirees, there are those who dedicated themselves wholeheartedly to their professional endeavors, investing years of hard work and offering nothing but their best. Despite not necessarily reaping significant financial rewards for their efforts, these individuals managed to successfully navigate the responsibilities of running their families.

Conversely, there exists a contrasting group characterized by corruption and a lack of sincere effort. These individuals, who often shirk hard work, have chosen the path of personal gain at the expense of ethical conduct. Their actions include lining their pockets through dubious means, creating a ripple effect that extends beyond their own lives. In a concerning turn of events, these individuals may find that their ill-gotten wealth only serves to burden society, particularly when it comes to the upbringing of their children.

The dichotomy between these two groups of retirees underscores the varied narratives that unfold during this phase of life. While some retire with a sense of fulfillment, having contributed earnestly to both their work and family life, others grapple with the consequences of unethical choices that cast shadows on their legacy and impact the wider community.

39. THE CRITIQUE

Some individuals seem to have a penchant for criticizing every action one takes. These individuals, characterized by their persistent inclination to criticize every action taken by others, often reveal more about themselves upon closer scrutiny of their critiques. A discerning analysis unveils a surprising revelation – a noticeable struggle on their part, particularly when it comes to even the most basic tasks. It becomes apparent that their ability to execute simple actions is impaired, raising questions about the credibility of their critiques.

Interestingly, it seems as though their primary vocation revolves around a rather negative aspect of interaction – the relentless identification and highlighting of flaws in others. Rather than engaging in constructive contributions or fostering a positive environment, they appear fixated on a pattern of fault-finding. This pattern not only reflects a limited constructive mindset but also hints at a potential inclination to deflect attention from their own shortcomings by focusing on those of others.

In essence, their habit of constant criticism may be a shield, protecting them from the vulnerability of their own imperfections. It becomes a coping mechanism, albeit an unhealthy one, as they navigate their own challenges by redirecting attention towards perceived shortcomings in those around them. Understanding this dynamic sheds light on the deeper motivations behind their behavior and emphasizes the importance of empathy and a more constructive approach to communication.

While constructive criticism can be valuable, an excess of unwarranted criticism can be detrimental. It not only diminishes motivation but also has the potential to sap the enthusiasm and drive of individuals. Those who make a career out of constant criticism run the risk of adversely impacting the lives of others, often leaving a trail of demotivated individuals in their wake.

40. THE FAÇADE OF WEALTH

Edwin and Emile resided as neighbors in the peaceful suburban landscape, their homes nestled amidst the tranquility of well-manicured lawns. Their shared domain boasted a sprawling expanse of greenery, meticulously tended to by both men. However, as autumn descended, a vibrant tapestry of leaves adorned their lawns, casting a picturesque yet daunting task before them.

Ever the diligent homeowner, Edwin wielded his trusty leaf blower with precision, swiftly banishing the autumnal debris from his verdant haven. Conversely, Emile's approach to lawn care was more laissez-faire; he addressed the foliage only in the early stages of autumn, leaving behind a patchwork of leaves that marred the otherwise pristine facade of his property.

Weeks passed, and the suburban landscape underwent a dramatic transformation as a blanket of snow enveloped the region. The once-vibrant lawns were now blanketed in a serene layer of white, imparting a uniform cleanliness to the entire neighborhood. Each house on the block exuded an air of tidiness, courtesy of nature's wintry intervention. However, as the thawing warmth of spring approached and the snow melted away, the familiar sight of scattered leaves resurfaced in Emile's lawn.

In the intricate tapestry of life, families emerge as unique compositions, each woven with diverse threads of values, principles, and experiences. Within this rich mosaic, some families stand as bastions of tradition and steadfastness, embracing discipline and philosophy as guiding lights that illuminate their path. They adhere to time-honored principles, instilling a sense of purpose and direction in their collective journey through life.

Contrastingly, other families traverse a more fragmented and ambiguous route, their tapestries woven with threads of uncertainty and ambiguity. Lacking the sturdy framework of discipline and philosophy, they navigate through life's complexities with varying degrees of coherence and cohesion. Their journey is marked by a patchwork of experiences, shaped by the ebb and flow of changing circumstances and values.

In this intricate interplay of familial dynamics, wealth often emerges as a double-edged sword. It is perceived as a glittering veil that conceals the imperfections and fractures within a family's structure. Wealth, with its material allure, can create an illusion of stability and harmony, masking underlying tensions and conflicts. Families bask in the glow of affluence, projecting an image of prosperity and success to the outside world.

However, this facade of wealth is not impervious to the passage of time and the winds of change. When the ephemeral veil of affluence fades, the true essence of a family's dynamics is laid bare for all to witness. The cracks in the facade become glaringly evident, revealing the raw emotions, conflicts, and insecurities that lie beneath the surface.

In these moments of reckoning, families are confronted with the stark reality of their internal dynamics. They are forced to confront their values, confront their relationships, and confront themselves. The transient nature of wealth fades into insignificance, as the true measure of a family's strength and resilience is revealed in their ability to navigate through adversity with grace and integrity.

Thus, in the tapestry of life, the interplay of wealth, values, and familial dynamics creates a complex and ever-evolving narrative. It is a story of contrasts, contradictions, and resilience, woven together by the shared experiences and aspirations of each unique family unit.

41. THE EARTHLY LIFE

Roger embarked on a journey to the city for a crucial business trip, initially enjoying a smooth ride along the highway. The highway passed through a small city. As he approached the city limits, his journey took an unexpected turn. Traffic congestion slowed his progress, exacerbated by ongoing construction work within the city. Despite his frustration, Roger found himself unable to escape the gridlock, forced to patiently navigate through the stop-and-go traffic. After enduring a seemingly endless half-hour of sluggish movement, Roger finally emerged from the confines of the city, relieved to find the traffic flowing smoothly once again. With a sense of determination, he pressed on and eventually arrived at his destination right on schedule.

Just as you can't escape a car stuck in slow or stopped traffic due to construction while driving, similarly, in life, once you're alive, you must continue on the path it takes you. Roger's journey serves as a reflection of the parallels between the challenges encountered on the road and those in life. Despite meticulous planning and sincere efforts, external circumstances may unexpectedly hinder our progress or halt it temporarily. In these moments, it's natural to feel overwhelmed and yearn for a quick solution.

At times, life unfolds in ways entirely different from what we expect or desire. It can feel as though time has slowed to a crawl or even come to a standstill, leaving us stranded in moments of frustration and uncertainty. In these challenging moments, it's natural to long for a swift resolution or for the world to offer some respite from its relentless pace.

Yet, amidst the trials and tribulations, it's crucial to hold onto the hope that tomorrow brings. Rather than being consumed by the immediate difficulties we face, it's essential to adopt a long-term perspective, considering where we envision ourselves not just in the coming days or months, but in the span of a decade or two.

By embracing this broader outlook, we can find solace in the knowledge that every setback, every obstacle, and every unexpected turn in our journey is merely a chapter in the larger narrative of our lives. Just as every twist and turn on a winding mountain road presents new surprises and challenges, so too does life offer its own array of unforeseen circumstances and opportunities.

In moments of doubt or despair, let us remind ourselves that the journey is not defined by its temporary setbacks, but by the resilience and determination with which we navigate its twists and turns. And as we continue along this winding road called life, may we find comfort in the knowledge that each bend in the path holds the promise of new adventures, growth, and ultimately, fulfillment.

42. LIVING FOR OTHERS

We often conceive of life as a pursuit driven solely by self-interest, a notion that seems technically sound at first glance. However, upon closer examination, it becomes evident that our existence is intricately intertwined with the lives of others. In reality, our worth, both tangible and intangible, is often determined by the perceptions and actions of those around us.

Consider the case of talent - be it in the arts, sports, or any other field. While an individual may possess innate abilities or cultivate multiple skills, the true value of these talents is realized only when they are shared with others. An actor, for instance, may possess remarkable acting prowess, but it is through the audience's appreciation and engagement that the full potential of their talent is actualized. In essence, the actor is not merely living for themselves; they are living to elicit emotions, provoke thoughts, and entertain others.

Similarly, the concept extends to more practical domains of life, such as agriculture and fishing. A farmer toils tirelessly to cultivate crops, and a fisherman braves the elements to haul in their catch. However, the fruits of their labor are not solely for their personal consumption. Instead, they are exchanged with others in a system of trade and commerce, ensuring that the products of their work reach a wider community. In this way, their livelihoods are not just about sustenance for themselves but also about contributing to the needs and desires of others.

Ultimately, while it may appear that we live for ourselves, the reality is far more nuanced. Our lives are intertwined with those of others, and our actions and contributions often ripple through society, shaping perceptions, experiences, and opportunities for both ourselves and those around us. We are not solitary entities navigating the world in isolation; rather, we are integral parts of a complex web of relationships and interdependencies, constantly influencing and being influenced by the collective tapestry of human existence.

43. ASSAULTING THE SPEAKER

A renowned professor, esteemed for his roles as both a scientist and a prolific writer, was invited to deliver a lecture at a prestigious Medical School known for its research endeavors. Throughout the talk, the professor gracefully fielded genuine inquiries from the audience, showcasing his expertise. However, a young faculty member began posing unrelated questions persistently, despite the professor's clear indication that they were outside his area of expertise. This behavior persisted, causing disruption throughout the lecture.

After the lecture concluded, attendees dispersed to their respective laboratories and study spaces. While traversing the corridors, I overheard the young faculty member boastfully claiming to have "confused" the distinguished professor during the talk. This faculty member had garnered a reputation for mistreating students and lacked a notable record of scholarly contributions, publishing infrequently. Despite subjecting her students to exhaustive workloads, often at the expense of public funding, little substantive output was produced.

Reflecting on a prior experience, I recalled presenting my research at another institution years earlier. Despite meticulous preparation and multiple rehearsals, I encountered an incompetent senior scientist who persistently questioned aspects of my work beyond its scope. Despite my repeated attempts to clarify, the scientist persisted in his line of inquiry.

The next day, a colleague from a different department, who had not attended my presentation, visited my office. Inquiring about any interactions with the senior scientist, I replied that I barely knew him. My colleague then recounted an incident in the cafeteria where the senior scientist and his associate, seated nearby, had engaged in a conversation. The associate had offered high praise for my presentation, however, the senior scientist expressed that he deliberately embarrassed me to humiliate in front of the audience and stated that he believed he had accomplished this goal.

Manipulating an audience is a simple task, particularly when many individuals lack expertise in the subject matter. When maliciously posed questions remain unanswered, audiences may wrongly perceive the speaker as lacking knowledge. Consequently, the speaker may face diminished respect and potential reluctance from others to collaborate.

It's crucial to acknowledge the effort speakers invest in preparing for presentations. Persistently asking questions beyond the speaker's expertise is akin to an assault, resulting in comparable societal consequences. Despite being the victim, both the speaker and the victim of assault may suffer societal disdain.

44. EXTRAVAGANT SPENDING OF TIME

Rodney, the son of a wealthy millionaire, struggled academically despite receiving special tutoring from numerous teachers throughout his schooling. Upon completing his college degree, tragedy struck as his father passed away, leaving Rodney the majority of his estate. With newfound wealth at his disposal, Rodney indulged in extravagant hobbies and surrounded himself with a large circle of friends. However, over time, he squandered his entire inheritance.

Many of us may not possess vast wealth like Rodney did, but we do have a wealth of time at our disposal. Currently, we have the freedom to spend our time as we please, indulging in various leisure activities such as watching television shows, movies, playing games, or simply listening to music for hours on end. However, this era of seemingly endless leisure may soon come to an end.

As the world progresses towards automation and artificial intelligence increasingly replaces human labor, our free time will diminish. We will be compelled to dedicate more time to study and self-improvement outside of our work hours. Gone will be the days when we could leisurely watch television or idly enjoy life without a care in the world. Time will become a scarce commodity, a luxury reserved for those who can afford it. In this rapidly changing landscape, the notion of having ample time by our side will become a thing of the past, and time itself will become a precious and valuable asset.

45. TRANSFER OF WEALTH

Ted and his younger sister Sabrina faced adversity from a tender age, having tragically lost their parents. As the eldest sibling, Ted took it upon himself to provide for and educate Sabrina, despite their meager resources. Through hard work and dedication, he managed to scrape together just enough to purchase a modest house, which he selflessly registered under Sabrina's name.

Ted's love for his sister knew no bounds, as evidenced by his decision to also register his small grocery business in her name. However, as time passed and Sabrina entered into marriage, the dynamics of their relationship took a distressing turn. Despite Ted's sacrifices and unwavering support, Sabrina, influenced perhaps by external pressures or changing priorities, eventually requested that Ted vacate the house they shared.

Adding insult to injury, she pursued legal action to seize control of Ted's business, leveraging the fact that it too was legally under her ownership. Forced to comply with the court's orders, Ted found himself stripped of both his home and livelihood, left to navigate the world with nothing but his principles and determination.

Undeterred by this betrayal and setback, Ted viewed this chapter of his life as a formative period, a training ground for the challenges that lay ahead. With resilience and an unwavering commitment to his values, he made the difficult decision to leave his past behind and start anew in a distant city.

Embracing humble beginnings, Ted took up odd jobs to make ends meet, all the while harboring a vision of building something greater from the ashes of his former life. Through sheer perseverance and a relentless work ethic, Ted's efforts bore fruit, culminating in the establishment of a thriving conglomerate that stood as a testament to his resilience and indomitable spirit.

Meanwhile, as time marched on, Sabrina found herself in dire straits, her once-promising future overshadowed by financial ruin. This stark reversal of fortune serves as a cautionary tale, highlighting the precarious nature of wealth and the potential pitfalls of its transfer.

In an ever-changing world where values and priorities evolve over time, the temptation to exploit inherited wealth or assets for personal gain can lead to unforeseen consequences. The next generation may not share the same reverence for hard-earned resources, risking their misuse or squandering in pursuit of short-term gains.

As such, it becomes imperative for individuals to exercise caution when transferring wealth, ensuring that it is done in a manner that safeguards against exploitation or mismanagement. By retaining control until after one's passing, individuals can mitigate the risk of their hard-earned assets falling into the wrong hands, preserving their legacy for future generations.

46. THE PRIORITY OF MAN CHANGES EVERY TEN YEARS

Throughout the course of a man's life, his priorities undergo a profound evolution, reshaping his desires and values every decade. What a baby yearns for at age one, such as comfort and nourishment, differs vastly from the aspirations of a five-year-old, who may seek adventure and exploration, or a ten-year-old, whose focus could shift towards friendship and belonging.

In earlier stages, basic needs like food and shelter may dominate, but as life progresses, material wealth and social status often take precedence. Health may be the priority after 60 years. However, as the twilight years approach, a spiritual yearning may emerge, reflecting a deeper quest for meaning and transcendence.

As the body inevitably succumbs to the passage of time, particularly around the age of 80 or when physical limitations inhibit the freedom of movement, the corporeal vessel becomes a confining prison for the mind's aspirations. It's during these moments that one longs to transcend earthly constraints, seeking solace in the promise of a heavenly abode where the spirit can roam free.

Moreover, man's value system is subject to flux over time. Initially embracing liberal ideals, he may gradually transition towards a more conservative stance as life experiences shape his perspectives and priorities. This metamorphosis reflects the intricate interplay between personal growth, societal influences, and the evolving landscape of human existence.

47. CHANGE OF GUARD

Titus, a dedicated CEO of his company for several decades, was adored by his employees for his compassionate approach. He made it a point to personally know each of his employees by name and would regularly engage with them across all departments, expressing genuine concern for their well-being. This fostered a strong sense of loyalty among the employees, who reciprocated Titus's care by putting in their best efforts, surpassing even neighboring companies in productivity.

However, tragedy struck when Titus fell ill and passed away, leaving his son Albert to inherit the CEO position. Unlike his father, Albert, despite his education from prestigious institutions, lacked interpersonal skills. He prioritized the company's financial statements and stock value above all else, neglecting the human aspect of running the business. Albert's focus solely on profit margins led to a disconnect with the employees, resulting in a hostile work environment where layoffs were frequent whenever profits fell short of expectations.

Under Albert's leadership, employees no longer felt valued, causing them to lose motivation and seek opportunities elsewhere. The decline in morale eventually took its toll on the company's financial stability, leading to a merger with another entity as a last resort. Thus, the once thriving company under Titus's leadership saw its downfall due to Albert's disregard for the well-being of its employees.

48. CONFRONTING ADVERSITY

The residents of Willow Oak Township had long harbored the desire to see a sturdy bridge stretching across the expansive river that traversed their land. Yet, constrained by meager resources, the township remained unable to materialize this dream for many years. Despite their limitations, the township leaders persevered tirelessly, until at last, they succeeded in erecting a bridge that connected their community.

However, the triumph of their achievement was soon tested by a powerful earthquake that struck several years later, causing significant damage to the newly built bridge. Undeterred by this setback, the township drew upon their prior experience in mobilizing financial and material resources, swiftly embarking on the construction of a new bridge engineered to withstand seismic activity. Through their resilience and determination, they ensured that the vital link connecting their township remained intact, ready to serve the needs of their community once more.

In the intricate fabric of existence, adversity is an inevitable thread woven into the very essence of human experience. From the unforeseen setbacks that threaten our financial stability to the sudden upheavals that shake the foundations of our homes, life presents us with myriad challenges that test our resolve and resilience. In these moments of trial, we stand at a crossroads, faced with a pivotal choice that will shape the course of our journey.

One path beckons us to surrender to the capricious hand of fate, resigning ourselves to the notion that defeat is an inescapable fate. It is a path laden with despair and disillusionment, where the weight of loss and disappointment threatens to engulf us in a sea of hopelessness. Yet, in the depths of despair, there lies another option—a path illuminated by the flickering flame of resilience and determination.

For those who dare to embrace this alternative, adversity becomes a crucible in which the alchemy of transformation occurs. They glean valuable lessons from their trials, forging an indomitable spirit that propels them forward with unwavering resolve. With each setback, they discover newfound strength and ingenuity, transforming setbacks into stepping stones toward greater heights of achievement.

It is through this journey of renewal and rebirth that the true essence of human potential is realized. Those who choose to start afresh emerge from the crucible of adversity not as mere survivors, but as architects of their own destiny. Empowered by their resilience, they embark on a journey of self-discovery and growth, unlocking hidden reserves of strength and courage that propel them to heights they once deemed unattainable.

In the face of adversity, we are presented with an opportunity—an opportunity to transcend our limitations, to redefine our boundaries, and to emerge from the crucible of hardship stronger, wiser, and more resilient than ever before. It is a journey fraught with challenges and uncertainties, yet it is also a journey filled with infinite possibilities and untapped potential. And for those who have the courage to seize it, the path to greatness awaits, illuminated by the unwavering light of resilience and determination.

49. THE LEMONADE SELLER

One sunny morning, Johann received a call from his friend, a bank manager, delivering the exhilarating news that he had officially crossed the threshold into billionaire status. It was a momentous occasion, marking the culmination of years of tireless work and strategic investment. Reflecting on his journey, Johann couldn't help but reminisce about the humble beginnings that laid the foundation for his remarkable success.

Johann and his sister Jane faced the harsh reality of losing their parents at a tender age, leaving them under the care of their loving grandparents. On their tenth birthday, amidst the simplicity of their upbringing, they were gifted twenty dollars. With youthful exuberance, they expressed their desire for a simple pleasure—a scoop of ice cream. However, their wise grandfather presented them with a choice that would plant the seeds of financial acumen in their young minds.

Instead of indulging in immediate gratification, their grandfather proposed the idea of investing in lemons for a lemonade stand at an upcoming marathon. Recognizing the potential for fun and profit, Johann and Jane eagerly agreed. With guidance from their grandfather, they learned the value of savvy spending by sourcing affordable lemons from a nearby farmer's market, maximizing their investment.

Their lemonade stand proved to be a resounding success, raking in a tidy profit of eighty dollars by the end of the day. Buoyed by this early taste of entrepreneurial success, the siblings ventured into a garden mowing business, offering their services to neighbors and continuing to apply their grandfather's teachings on financial prudence.

As they grew older, Johann and Jane's entrepreneurial endeavors expanded, guided by their grandfather's sage advice to diversify their investments. They ventured into the realm of technology stocks, harnessing their combined business acumen to navigate the volatile market landscape. In parallel, they remained committed to their community, allocating a portion of their earnings to support a local old age home where they volunteered their time and efforts.

Johann's exceptional academic achievements and dedication to social impact earned him a full scholarship to a prestigious university, where he further honed his skills and expanded his network. Alongside his like-minded peers, he co-founded a small tech company, laying the groundwork for future success. Their groundbreaking product caught the attention of a larger corporation, resulting in a lucrative acquisition that injected substantial capital into their burgeoning enterprise.

With a shrewd eye for emerging technologies and a penchant for strategic investments, Johann's ventures flourished, catapulting him to the pinnacle of financial success. As the stock prices of his tech companies soared, Johann's net worth skyrocketed, culminating in his extraordinary journey from modest beginnings to billionaire status—a testament to the transformative power of resilience, perseverance, and the enduring lessons imparted by his beloved grandfather.

50. STRATEGIC LEADERSHIP IN GOVERNANCE: LESSONS FROM A VICE CHANCELLOR

During Prof. KG Adiyodi's tenure as Vice Chancellor of Cochin University of Science and Technology (CUSAT), the institution flourished with ample funds supporting its myriad programs, a feat that left both students and faculty in awe. The enigma surrounding the source of these funds was finally unveiled when the Vice Chancellor orchestrated an event inviting a Central Minister to inaugurate several new departments within the university.

As the inauguration unfolded, the Central Minister took to the podium, revealing insights into the typical plight of Vice Chancellors across the country who often found themselves scrambling for resources in their visits to New Delhi. However, he remarked on the stark contrast presented by Prof. KG Adiyodi, who approached his interactions with a strategic finesse that transcended mere requests for favors. Instead, the Vice Chancellor would eloquently present the ongoing and prospective programs at CUSAT, capturing the attention and support of key senior secretaries within the Ministry.

Prior to meeting the Central Minister, Prof. Adiyodi would meticulously engage with these senior secretaries, articulating his visionary projects and garnering their endorsement. This proactive approach not only secured vital assistance but also fostered a network of support that propelled CUSAT to new heights of excellence.

Expanding beyond academia, the principles embodied by Prof. Adiyodi's approach resonate in broader spheres of leadership and governance. Elected representatives, be they Members of Parliament or Senators, shoulder a triad of responsibilities: nurturing the economic vitality of their constituencies, crafting legislation conducive to national progress, and cultivating diplomatic ties with foreign nations. Mere rhetorical flourish within parliamentary chambers or ceremonial engagements within their constituencies fall short of fulfilling these mandates.

True efficacy lies in the diligent cultivation of relationships with bureaucrats and entrepreneurs to establish a robust economic framework. Additionally, legislators must engage with constituents to identify legislative priorities that reflect the needs and aspirations of the populace. Simultaneously, they must actively participate in committees and diplomatic endeavors to forge alliances and strengthen international relations.

In essence, effective leadership transcends superficial gestures, requiring a strategic and proactive approach that engages stakeholders, navigates bureaucratic channels, and fosters meaningful collaborations both domestically and on the global stage. Prof. KG Adiyodi's legacy serves as a beacon of this transformative leadership, illuminating pathways toward progress and prosperity.

51. NAVIGATING LIFE'S POTHOLES

As Harry navigated his car along the bustling road, he encountered an unexpected obstacle: a daunting pothole directly in his path. A split-second decision loomed before him. Should he slam on the brakes and risk being rear-ended by the vehicle trailing closely behind, or should he brave the discomfort of the pothole and forge ahead? With a quick assessment of the situation, he opted for the latter, guiding his car cautiously over the rough terrain, much to the chagrin of his passengers, who were jolted by the unexpected bump.

This scenario on the road mirrors life's journey in many ways. Just as Harry faced a sudden challenge while driving, we too encounter unforeseen obstacles along our path. Despite our best efforts to navigate safely, there are times when circumstances beyond our control force us to make tough decisions, often sacrificing comfort for the sake of avoiding greater harm.

However, it is in these moments of adversity that our resilience is truly tested. Like Harry maneuvering through the pothole, our ability to rise from setbacks and continue forward defines our strength and resilience. Every stumble, every fall, serves as an opportunity for growth and learning. It is through overcoming adversity that we cultivate the resilience needed to persevere in the face of life's challenges.

Indeed, the journey of life is not always smooth sailing. But it is through navigating the rough patches, weathering the storms, and rising from the falls that we emerge stronger, wiser, and ultimately, more successful. As we embrace the lessons learned from each obstacle overcome, we pave the way for a brighter, more resilient future.

52. STAYING RELEVANT

Several decades ago, Mr. Henry embarked on a journey to revolutionize transportation with his groundbreaking creation - the automobile. His earliest models were humble in design, embodying simplicity and functionality. However, as time progressed, Mr. Henry's visionary company embarked on a relentless pursuit of innovation, constantly pushing the boundaries of automotive technology.

Through relentless research and development efforts, Mr. Henry's company introduced a myriad of enhancements to their vehicles. From the introduction of essential features like windshield wipers and heating systems to the integration of luxuries such as air conditioning and radio systems, each iteration of their automobiles represented a leap forward in comfort, convenience, and performance. Not content with mere comfort, the company also focused on enhancing the power and safety of their vehicles, equipping them with powerful engines and advanced braking systems.

As the new millennium dawned, Mr. Henry's company embraced the global shift towards sustainability and environmental consciousness by transitioning to electric vehicles. This bold move not only showcased their commitment to innovation but also positioned them as pioneers in the era of clean energy transportation.

Looking ahead to the future, Mr. Henry's company is poised to once again revolutionize the automotive industry with the development of autonomous vehicles. By leveraging cutting-edge technologies such as artificial intelligence and machine learning, they aim to redefine the concept of mobility, offering safer, more efficient transportation solutions for the modern world.

Reflecting on the evolution of Mr. Henry's company, one can draw parallels to the career journey of individuals starting out in the workforce. Just as Mr. Henry continuously adapted and improved his automobiles to stay ahead of the curve, professionals must also embrace a mindset of lifelong learning and adaptability to thrive in today's rapidly evolving technological landscape.

Thirty years ago, when many of us began our careers, the skills and knowledge acquired in school formed the foundation of our professional expertise. However, in an era defined by constant technological advancement, static knowledge quickly becomes obsolete. To remain relevant and competitive, individuals must commit themselves to ongoing skill development and staying abreast of emerging technologies.

In the dynamic landscape of the modern workplace, complacency is not an option. Companies that fail to innovate and evolve risk being left behind in an increasingly competitive market. Just as Mr. Henry's company continuously improved its products to meet the evolving needs of consumers, organizations must prioritize innovation and adaptation to ensure their long-term viability.

In essence, whether it's navigating the ever-changing terrain of technological innovation or steering the course of one's career, the key to success lies in embracing change, continuously learning, and striving for progress. Just as Mr. Henry's legacy endures through his groundbreaking contributions to the automotive industry, so too can individuals and organizations leave their mark by embracing innovation and embracing change.

53. DEFINING FACTORS

After years of arduous negotiation, a small country successfully secured a substantial loan from the World Bank to finance the construction of a vital bridge. This ambitious project was seen as a crucial step in bolstering the country's infrastructure and facilitating economic growth. However, what began as a promising endeavor soon turned into a cautionary tale of mismanagement and deceit.

The construction contract for the bridge was awarded to a company with close ties to the president, sparking allegations of nepotism and corruption. Despite protests and concerns raised by experts in the field, the president's friend was granted the tender, and construction commenced without further delay.

Years passed, and the completed bridge stood as a symbol of progress and development. However, cracks began to appear both literally and figuratively. Reports emerged of structural deficiencies and alarming signs of instability. Upon closer inspection, it was discovered that substandard materials, particularly inferior quality steel, had been used in the construction process.

The revelation sent shockwaves through the nation, prompting outrage and calls for accountability. The bridge, once hailed as a triumph of engineering, now posed a grave risk to public safety. With no other recourse, authorities made the difficult decision to demolish the bridge, erasing years of effort and investment in a matter of days.

This unfortunate incident serves as a stark reminder of the importance of integrity and competence in infrastructure projects of such magnitude. It underscores the need for rigorous oversight and adherence to quality standards to ensure the safety and durability of public infrastructure.

The analogy of using different qualities of steel for distinct purposes extends beyond construction to the realm of human endeavors and personal development. Just as specific grades of steel are chosen for their suitability in different applications, individuals possess unique qualities and aptitudes that shape their paths in life.

Consider a graduating class, where students may appear similar on the surface but diverge in their journeys and achievements over time. A student who pursues a career in law enforcement may possess different attributes and experiences compared to one who becomes a scholar or educator. Similarly, those who ascend to positions of leadership in multinational corporations will exhibit distinct qualities from those who navigate the bureaucratic landscape of government service.

Ultimately, just as the quality of materials determines the strength and resilience of a structure, the qualities and choices of individuals shape their destinies and contributions to society. It is through recognizing and nurturing these differences that we can collectively build a more vibrant and resilient future.

54. THE SUCCESSFUL CEO IN THE BOARDROOM

Once upon a time in a distant kingdom, a wise king found himself confronted with the inevitable passage of time. With his reign drawing to a close, he pondered the future of his realm, seeking the most worthy successor among his two sons.

To test their mettle and discern the one fit to wear the crown, the king devised a challenging task. The agricultural lands surrounding two vital villages were beleaguered by herds of marauding deer and ferocious boars, wreaking havoc upon the livelihoods of the villagers. Determined to confront this threat, the king decreed that whichever prince could rid the land of these pests within five days would ascend to the throne.

Equipped with only a modest entourage of five soldiers with chariots and a single bullock cart, the princes set out to fulfill their father's command. The elder son, fueled by ambition and armed with foresight, opted to load the cart with a plethora of bows and arrows, anticipating a protracted battle. Meanwhile, the younger prince, guided by a different strategy, chose to carry only a meager supply of arrows, trusting in his resourcefulness and agility to see him through.

As the days passed and the hunt unfolded, it became apparent that the elder prince's meticulous preparation and abundance of ammunition afforded him a significant advantage. With a relentless barrage of arrows, he swiftly decimated the ranks of the troublesome beasts, earning him the admiration of the villagers and the favor of his father.

Upon the successful completion of the task, the elder prince was duly anointed as the new ruler of the kingdom, his victory a testament to his cunning and prowess. And thus, under his reign, the land flourished anew, blessed with a leader worthy of the crown.

When a CEO strides into the boardroom, it is not just his presence that commands attention, but the tangible and intangible achievements he carries with him, reflections of his team's collective efforts throughout the year. A skilled CEO understands that his role extends far beyond mere management; it is about fostering a culture of excellence, motivating individuals, and guiding the company toward its goals.

As he stands before the board, a successful CEO adeptly weaves a narrative of progress and innovation. He proudly showcases the trophies and accolades earned by his team, tangible symbols of their dedication and hard work. Each award represents not just a milestone, but a testament to the collaborative spirit and ingenuity that defines the company.

But it is not just about past victories; a visionary CEO also paints a compelling picture of the future. With unwavering confidence, he articulates his vision for the company's trajectory over the next 5, 10, or even 20 years. Drawing upon strategic insights and market trends, he outlines ambitious growth plans, highlighting key initiatives and investments that will propel the company forward.

In addition to celebrating past successes and charting a course for the future, a truly effective CEO understands the importance of motivation and encouragement. With genuine enthusiasm, he acknowledges the contributions of each team member, inspiring them to reach even greater heights. Whether through words of praise or opportunities for professional development, he fosters a culture where every individual feels valued and empowered to excel.

In the boardroom, the CEO is not just a leader, but a visionary, strategist, and motivator rolled into one. Armed with accomplishments, insights, and a clear vision for the future, he commands the respect and admiration of the board, instilling confidence in the company's continued success.

55. WORKING EFFORTLESSLY

In the past, Bart adhered to a rigid routine of meticulously tending to his lawn every weekend throughout spring and summer. Armed with his trusty lawn mower, he diligently moved across the expanse of greenery, methodically gathering the freshly shorn grass in the mower's grass bag. However, this seemingly straightforward task was burdened with its own set of challenges. As Bart progressed, the bag would inevitably reach its capacity, prompting him to interrupt his rhythm and trudge to the yard's edge for the laborious process of emptying it. Sometimes, frustratingly, the lawn mower would sputter to a halt just before the bag reached its limit, adding an extra layer of annoyance to an already arduous chore.

Bart's dissatisfaction with this routine came to a head one day as he observed a neighbor effortlessly manicuring his own lawn. Unlike Bart, the neighbor eschewed the use of a grass bag, opting instead to let the clippings scatter naturally across the lawn. Bart's epiphany struck him like a bolt of lightning. Suddenly, he comprehended the inefficiency of his approach—constantly interrupting his mowing to deal with a cumbersome grass bag, all the while expending unnecessary energy and time.

With newfound determination, Bart decided to adopt his neighbor's method. Casting aside the grass bag, he powered through his lawn with renewed vigor, allowing the clippings to fall where they may. Freed from the shackles of the grass bag, Bart discovered a newfound efficiency in his lawn maintenance routine. Not only did he complete the task in record time, but he also found himself less fatigued, able to relish in the satisfaction of a job well done without the burdensome interruptions of emptying a grass bag.

At times, the tasks we undertake can feel burdensome and monotonous, draining our energy and testing our patience. The repetitive nature of certain work can lead to feelings of frustration and exhaustion. However, within this realm of monotony lies the potential for transformation. By reevaluating our tactics and approaches, we can unlock new paths towards efficiency and ease.

Consider this: what if the key to completing a task effortlessly lies not in the task itself, but in our approach to it? Often, we become entrenched in familiar methods, even when they prove to be inefficient or laborious. Yet, by daring to challenge these norms, we open ourselves to the possibility of a smoother, more streamlined workflow.

Imagine a scenario where a once-tedious chore becomes a breeze simply by altering our tactics. Whether it's breaking down the task into smaller, more manageable chunks, utilizing new tools or technologies, or even shifting our mindset to embrace a different perspective, the potential for improvement is vast.

By embracing this philosophy of adaptability and innovation, we empower ourselves to navigate the challenges of our work with newfound ease. No longer bound by the constraints of tradition or habit, we pave the way for a future where even the most daunting tasks can be conquered effortlessly.

56. ANERGIC BEHAVIOR IS DETRIMENTAL TO STUDENTS, WORKERS AND EXECUTIVES

In immunology, anergy delineates a profound state of unresponsiveness observed in T cells, persisting despite repeated attempts at stimulation. This phenomenon underscores a crucial aspect of the immune system's regulatory mechanisms, where T cells, pivotal orchestrators of immune responses, exhibit a remarkable tolerance or indifference towards encountered antigens. At its core, anergy reflects a state of functional paralysis within T cells, wherein they fail to mount the requisite immune response, even when confronted with antigens that would typically trigger activation. This state arises through diverse molecular mechanisms, prominently involving alterations in signaling pathways crucial for T cell activation. Notably, anergy induction often involves the disruption of key signaling events initiated upon T cell receptor (TCR) engagement, thereby impeding the downstream cascade of events necessary for full T cell activation.

Anergic behavior extends beyond the realms of immunology to permeate various facets of human endeavor, including academia, the workforce, and corporate leadership. In these contexts, anergic behavior manifests as a state of diminished responsiveness or engagement, akin to the immunological concept but applied to social and professional dynamics.

In academic settings, students may display anergic behavior when they exhibit a lack of enthusiasm or motivation despite exposure to stimulating educational materials or learning opportunities. This can manifest as disinterest in classroom activities, passive participation, or a reluctance to engage with course content, even when presented with intellectually stimulating challenges.

Similarly, within the workforce, employees may demonstrate anergic behavior characterized by a lack of initiative, reduced productivity, or disengagement from their professional responsibilities despite providing incentives and good salary. This could stem from various factors, including burnout, lethargy, dissatisfaction with work conditions, or a mismatch between personal aspirations and career trajectories.

At the executive level, anergic behavior may manifest in leaders who exhibit a passive approach to decision-making, a reluctance to innovate, or a failure to inspire and mobilize their teams effectively in spite of repeated feedback. In such cases, the organization may experience stagnation, missed opportunities for growth, or a decline in overall performance due to the inertia induced by anergic leadership.

The underlying mechanisms driving anergic behavior in these contexts are multifaceted and often intersect with psychological, social, and organizational factors. For instance, chronic stress, job dissatisfaction, or a lack of clear goals and feedback mechanisms can contribute to the development of anergic tendencies among students, workers, or executives.

Addressing anergic behavior in these domains requires a holistic approach that addresses underlying root causes while fostering environments conducive to engagement, motivation, and productivity. This may involve implementing strategies such as mentorship programs, wellness initiatives, professional development opportunities, or organizational restructuring aimed at promoting a sense of purpose, autonomy, and belonging.

By recognizing and addressing anergic behavior across diverse spheres of human activity, we can cultivate environments that nurture creativity, productivity, and fulfillment, ultimately fostering individual growth and collective success.

57. EXPERIENCE MATTERS

Alena's heart brimmed with anticipation and joy as she eagerly awaited the arrival of her cherished family, journeying from a distant city to reunite with her. Fueled by excitement, she resolved to orchestrate a culinary extravaganza befitting the occasion, settling on her beloved specialty, chicken tikka masala. This gastronomic marvel was a testament to her culinary prowess, boasting a harmonious fusion of spices and other ingredients meticulously curated to tantalize the taste buds. Alena understood the pivotal importance of achieving the perfect balance of flavors, knowing it would leave an indelible impression on her guests' palates.

With determination fueling her every move, Alena embarked on her culinary odyssey, transforming her kitchen into a symphony of aromas. Each spice contributed its unique essence to the melodic ensemble, as Alena expertly orchestrated the cooking process with practiced finesse. Her hands moved with precision and grace, skillfully blending the spices and vegetables to coax out their fullest flavors, ensuring that every component harmonized flawlessly.

When her family finally descended upon her home, the air crackled with anticipation as they eagerly gathered around the table. With each delectable bite of Alena's culinary masterpiece, their taste buds were transported to new realms of delight. Despite their attempts to decipher the intricate blend of spices, they found themselves enchanted by the dish's elusive allure. Each mouthful unfolded like a symphony of flavors, a sensory journey that left them yearning for more.

Experience is akin to the spices in Alena's chicken tikka masala. In the realm of project management, experience serves as the cornerstone of success, regardless of the endeavor's scale or complexity. It is the culmination of knowledge and insights gleaned from past undertakings that empowers professionals to navigate challenges with confidence and finesse. Even the most modest projects can evolve into resounding triumphs when entrusted to seasoned individuals armed with a wealth of expertise.

The depth and breadth of one's experience often dictate the outcome of their endeavors. With each project embarked upon, professionals accumulate a treasure trove of insights, refining their approaches and honing their skills. These cumulative experiences act as a guiding light, illuminating the path towards innovative solutions and efficient strategies, irrespective of the project's intricacies.

As projects increase in magnitude, the significance of experience becomes even more pronounced. While novices may stumble in the face of adversity, seasoned veterans draw upon their extensive repertoire of past triumphs and setbacks to navigate challenges with poise and determination. Thus, it is through the crucible of experience that individuals elevate their capabilities, ensuring the success of every undertaking they pursue.

58. PASSION TRIUMPHS

Filippo Brunelleschi stands as the pioneering figure in Renaissance architecture, credited with revolutionizing the field. His crowning achievement, the dome of the Florence Cathedral, Santa Maria del Fiore, is an enduring symbol of his ingenuity and vision. Remarkably, Brunelleschi embarked on this monumental project with no prior experience in constructing large domes.

Driven by a potent blend of skill, innovation, and an unwavering passion for both engineering and art, Brunelleschi embarked on a journey that would redefine architectural possibilities. His meticulous attention to detail, coupled with groundbreaking technological advancements, allowed him to surmount challenges that had confounded his predecessors.

Brunelleschi's mastery extended beyond the mere physical construction of structures; he possessed a profound understanding of aesthetics and spatial harmony, infusing his designs with a sense of grandeur and elegance. His daring innovations not only transformed the skyline of Florence but also inspired generations of architects and engineers to push the boundaries of their craft.

Passion consistently prevails over both experience and wealth. Time and again, individuals driven by an intense passion for their pursuits outshine those who rely solely on their accumulated years of experience or the resources afforded by wealth. Passion fuels relentless determination, propelling individuals to push beyond their limits, continuously educate themselves, embrace challenges, and innovate in ways that experience alone cannot dictate.

Moreover, passion infuses endeavors with a profound sense of purpose, igniting a fire within individuals that transcends material concerns. While experience undoubtedly contributes valuable insights and wealth provides access to resources, it is passion that serves as the driving force behind remarkable achievements.

History is replete with examples of passionate individuals who have defied the odds and reshaped the world. From inventors who revolutionized industries to artists who captured the human experience with unparalleled depth, their unwavering dedication to their craft propelled them to greatness.

Passion is the ultimate catalyst for success, transcending the limitations of experience and wealth to unlock boundless potential. It is the driving force that propels individuals to defy convention, challenge the status quo, and leave an indelible mark on the world.

59. TRANSITIONING TO RETIREMENT YEARS

After a long day at school, Savio eagerly headed to the nearby football field to indulge in his favorite pastime. The afternoon sun bathed the field in a warm glow as Savio kicked the ball with friends, reveling in the freedom of play.

Upon returning home, his mother greeted him with a refreshing bath to wash away the day's sweat and grime. As he emerged, clean and rejuvenated, she presented him with a bowl brimming with plump, juicy grapes. Savio's eyes lit up at the sight, and he eagerly accepted the delicious treat.

Settling down in front of the television, Savio immersed himself in the colorful world of his favorite cartoon characters. With each bite of the succulent grapes, his enjoyment doubled, the sweetness of the fruit complementing the whimsical antics on the screen.

However, as he reached the bottom of the bowl, his excitement waned. The grapes nestled there, having lost their freshness, failed to match the lusciousness of their counterparts.

In the broader scope of life, Savio's experiences echoed a universal truth: the abundance of resources available to us in our youth often dwindles in retirement. Yet, as retirement approaches, the landscape shifts, and the certainty of financial stability can give way to uncertainty. The nest egg carefully cultivated over decades may suddenly seem insufficient to cover the expenses of life's twilight years.

Savio's story serves as a poignant reminder of the importance of foresight and prudent planning. Just as he savored each grape, cherishing its sweetness before it faded, so too must we cherish and wisely utilize the resources available to us today. Whether it be through diligent saving, prudent investments, or cultivating meaningful relationships, the choices we make in the present shape the security of our future.

In embracing this wisdom, we honor the essence of Savio's journey—a journey marked by the appreciation of life's simple pleasures and the foresight to prepare for the uncertainties that lie ahead. It is through this mindful approach to living that we can ensure a more secure and fulfilling tomorrow, regardless of the twists and turns that life may bring.

60. IF YOU DO NOT LEAD YOUR LIFE, YOU WILL SURRENDER TO OTHERS

Fabian found himself amidst a ticking clock, with just two days left to submit a captivating picture for a prestigious contest. His father, ever the resourceful guide, suggested a forest just a half-hour drive from their home, promising breathtaking scenery illuminated by the morning sun's gentle rays. Eager to seize the opportunity, Fabian agreed to the plan, envisioning the perfect shot in his mind's eye.

As dawn broke on the appointed day, Fabian's father dutifully attempted to rouse his slumbering son. Yet, Fabian's desire for more sleep battled fiercely against his aspirations. After a persistent half-hour of cajoling, Fabian reluctantly stirred from his dreams, begrudgingly realizing the value of seizing the moment.

Their journey to the forest was a lesson in patience, with a meandering single lane and a procession of cars obstructing their path. Trapped behind a slow-moving vehicle driven by an elderly individual, Fabian's father imparted a timeless truth: "However talented you are, if you are not disciplined, and if you do not take charge of your life, you'll find yourself at the mercy of others' whims."

Arriving at the forest hours behind schedule, the enchanting spectacle that had beckoned them was but a fleeting memory. Nevertheless, they made the best of the situation, capturing what remained of the scenery and submitting their efforts to the contest with hopes still intact.

Disappointment loomed as Fabian's submission failed to clinch victory. The coveted first place was claimed by none other than Fabian's own classmate, whose photograph of a tree-lined street bathed in the early morning light echoed the vision initially proposed by Fabian's father, albeit in a different setting.

In the aftermath, amidst the sting of defeat, Fabian gleaned a poignant lesson: that seizing opportunities when they arise is paramount, for in the ebb and flow of life, hesitation can cost one dearly.

61. PROSPERITY THROUGH INDIVIDUAL CONTRIBUTION

In Guilio's expansive backyard, a symphony of apple trees flourished under his attentive care. With a meticulous routine, he nourished his orchard, administering fertilizer twice a year, diligently combating pests with targeted insecticides, and providing hydration during parched summer spells devoid of rain. As a testament to his nurturing touch, each tree boasted a verdant canopy, bursting forth with a bountiful harvest of crisp apples come late summer.

Merely a stone's throw away from Guilio's verdant domain stood Peter's modest abode, where a solitary apple tree languished in neglect. Despite its potential, Peter's lackadaisical approach to cultivation resulted in a sorry sight. The tree, adorned with withered foliage, offered scant blossoms in the spring and yielded diminutive, misshapen fruits come summertime.

In the broader context of societal dynamics, the analogy between Guilio's thriving orchard and the ideal functioning of a nation becomes evident. A nation prospers when its citizens, akin to the leaves of Guilio's trees, contribute abundantly to its collective well-being. Just as the health of the leaves determines the quality of the fruit they bear, the vitality and productivity of individuals shape the prosperity of a nation.

In essence, a thriving society mirrors Guilio's meticulously tended orchard, where diligent care and nurturing yield a rich harvest. Conversely, neglect and apathy, exemplified by Peter's neglected tree, lead to stunted growth and meager returns. Thus, the success of a nation hinges upon the conscientious efforts of its citizens, who, like Guilio, must cultivate their potential to ensure a flourishing and fruitful society.

62. THE GOLD NUGGET

While vacationing in a national park, Danny's eyes widened as he stumbled upon a large gold nugget glinting amidst the earth. According to park regulations, he was entitled to keep his serendipitous find. Considering the skyrocketing price of gold, Danny's mind immediately leaped to the prospect of selling the nugget. His initial plan involved melting it down into a sleek gold bar for sale.

However, just before executing his plan, Danny decided to seek advice from a seasoned goldsmith. To his surprise, the goldsmith revealed that nuggets often fetched higher prices at auction houses due to their rarity and unique characteristics. Trusting the expert's insight, Danny opted to take a different route. He consigned the nugget to an esteemed auction house. Danny got a significant sum for his gold nugget, more than he would have received if he had sold it as a gold bar.

The manner in which you promote your product influences its perceived worth. Transitioning from personal success to professional prowess, it is crucial to recognize the importance of a meticulously crafted curriculum vitae (CV), especially when aiming for executive or management roles. Despite a wealth of experience and accomplishments garnered through years of dedication in various roles, the CV serves as the gateway for potential employers to gauge one's suitability for the desired position.

Crafting a compelling CV is akin to painting a masterpiece, where every stroke and hue contributes to the overall impression. It's not merely a mundane task of listing experiences and qualifications but an art form that demands creativity, precision, and strategic thinking.

At its core, a well-crafted CV is a reflection of one's professional identity—a carefully curated narrative that encapsulates achievements, skills, and aspirations. Like an artist selecting the perfect palette, a job seeker must carefully choose the content and format of their CV to resonate with potential employers.

Moreover, writing a CV involves more than just showcasing qualifications; it requires storytelling prowess. Each section of the CV should weave together a cohesive narrative that communicates the candidate's journey, from academic endeavors to professional milestones. Just as a skilled storyteller captivates their audience, a compelling CV captivates recruiters, drawing them into the candidate's narrative and leaving a lasting impression.

Furthermore, the art of CV writing extends beyond mere presentation—it delves into the realm of strategy. Every word, bullet point, and formatting choice should be deliberate, aimed at positioning the candidate as the ideal fit for the desired role. Just as an artist considers the composition of their masterpiece, a job seeker must consider the layout, tone, and content of their CV to effectively convey their value proposition.

In this competitive landscape, the CV must transcend mere enumeration of achievements; it should articulate a narrative that reflects the depth and breadth of one's capabilities. Every milestone, no matter how seemingly mundane, contributes to the mosaic of expertise that defines an individual's professional journey. Companies scrutinize every detail, seeking indicators of leadership, innovation, and problem-solving prowess.

In essence, the CV is not merely a document but a strategic tool, meticulously tailored to align with the company's objectives and showcase the candidate's potential to drive success. Therefore, it's imperative to invest time and effort in crafting a CV that not only highlights accomplishments but also conveys the essence of one's professional persona. After all, in the realm of executive recruitment, the margin for error is slim, and every word on the CV carries the weight of potential opportunity.

63. BETTER STAY LONELY AT THE TOP THAN IN THE DITCH

From the moment life emerges, the inevitable return to the earth awaits every organism. Within the intricate tapestry of existence lies the food web, a complex dance where predators stalk their prey. Among these predators, man stands as the apex, wielding intellect and skill to dominate. Yet, even in this supremacy, mortality remains an ever-present specter. Whether through the silent onslaught of infectious diseases, the insidious creep of cancer, the consequences of lifestyle choices, or the immutable hand of genetics, death lurks as an equalizer, leveling even the mightiest.

Success, too, breeds its own challenges. Within the structured confines of organizations or the broader realms of society, attaining a position of influence or prominence often invites envy and ambition. Those who covet your stature, whether driven by jealousy or ambition, will eagerly seek opportunities to undermine you. Their agendas are clandestine, waiting patiently for the perfect moment to strike. They may cloak their intentions in seemingly innocent gestures, such as urging a teetotaler to partake in revelry at a celebration. Yet, succumbing to such temptations can set a perilous course toward failure later in life.

At the helm of an organization, vigilance becomes paramount. Beneath the guise of friendship and goodwill, adversaries may lurk, biding their time to exploit vulnerabilities. Trust becomes a scarce commodity, and discretion a shield against betrayal. It is wiser to maintain a cautious distance from those who seek proximity solely for personal gain.

In the lofty heights of success, solitude often becomes the companion of choice. It is preferable to stand alone at the summit than to find oneself abandoned in the depths of despair. In this solitude lies a sanctuary, a refuge from the treacheries that abound below.

64. IMPORTANCE OF CONTINUING EDUCATION

In bygone eras, completing one's final examinations often felt like the end of a journey, a symbolic tossing of textbooks into the river. Once gainfully employed, the expectation was simple: follow management's directives without much need for ongoing learning. However, the landscape has since transformed dramatically.

Today, the necessity of continuous education cannot be overstated. Remaining relevant in the workforce demands a commitment to perpetual learning, lest one risk becoming obsolete and phased out. This imperative applies across diverse sectors, from management and technical professions to business, medicine, and even agriculture. To thrive in any role, individuals must stay abreast of the latest technological advancements shaping their respective fields.

While management may set the course, there's an implicit expectation for employees to not only execute current tasks but also to anticipate and advocate for future innovations that could propel the organization forward. In an era where stagnation spells doom for businesses, proactive learning becomes not just advantageous but essential for survival for the people and organizations.

Gone are the days of sporadic knowledge updates; in today's hyper connected world, staying informed is an everyday pursuit. With global literacy rates and the number of advanced degrees reaching unprecedented highs, information dissemination has become instantaneous. Technological breakthroughs occurring in remote corners of the globe are broadcast worldwide within minutes, underscoring the urgency for continuous education.

Moreover, demographic shifts, coupled with advancements in medicine, have prolonged lifespans, leading to extended working lives. Retirement is no longer synonymous with complete disengagement; instead, many individuals seek meaningful avenues for continued contribution and personal fulfillment.

In essence, the importance of continuing education transcends individual career trajectories—it is the cornerstone of societal progress and organizational resilience in an ever-evolving world. Embracing a mindset of lifelong learning isn't just a professional obligation; it's a strategic imperative for navigating the complexities of modernity and securing a prosperous future.

65. ZERO TO HERO

Zero is often regarded as a symbol of humiliation and defeat. Whether it is receiving a zero on an exam or seeing a zero balance in your bank account, it can feel like a personal setback.

Jarrett experienced this firsthand when he received a zero on his math examination. Faced with two choices, either maintain the status quo or work diligently. Jarrett decided to confront the challenge head-on. Through sheer determination and daily practice, Jarrett transformed his academic performance, eventually achieving top grades in his school. That initial zero became the catalyst for his remarkable improvement.

Similarly, Shirley encountered adversity when she sat for an entrance test that penalized incorrect answers with negative marks. Despite her hard work and preparation, she ended up with a zero on the test. Surprisingly, the organization, recognizing the widespread struggle of the candidates, admitted students with scores ranging from zero upwards.

Brian faced a different kind of crisis when his bank account hit zero, leading to the loss of his business and home. Undeterred, Brian tapped into his resilience and creativity to rebuild what he had lost. Over time, his business flourished into a thriving conglomerate. Proudly, Brian would regale his friends with stories of how he had started from zero and built his empire from scratch.

In the realm of academia, individuals who receive a grade of zero often find themselves subjected to ridicule, with comparisons drawn to the image of an egg—a symbol of fragility and emptiness. However, amidst this mockery, zero holds a profound significance as a beacon of hope and potential.

Yet, beneath the surface lies a different narrative. Zero, paradoxically, embodies the essence of possibility and renewal. Like the fertile void from which life emerges, a zero grade signifies a blank canvas upon which one can paint a new trajectory. It serves as a catalyst for introspection, prompting individuals to reassess their approach, identify areas for growth, and embark on a journey of self-improvement.

Moreover, zero symbolizes the resilience of the human spirit in the face of adversity. Just as a seed lying dormant in the soil holds the promise of future growth, so too does a zero grade serve as a catalyst for transformation. Through perseverance, dedication, and unwavering determination, individuals can transcend the limitations imposed by their initial setbacks, forging a path towards academic success and personal fulfillment.

Thus, while the specter of ridicule may loom large, those confronted with a zero grade are reminded of the inherent power of hope. In the crucible of adversity, they discover the resilience to rise above their circumstances, embracing the boundless potential that lies within. In this way, zero emerges not as a mark of defeat, but as a harbinger of possibility—a testament to the indomitable human spirit and its capacity for growth and renewal.

66. RESURRECTING GRANDEUR

Once, amidst the hustle and bustle of the automobile workshop, a classic 1960 Cadillac stood quietly, its sleek lines and vintage allure captivating all who beheld it. The owner had entrusted it to the care of the mechanics, hoping to revive its former glory. However, the passage of time proved unkind, as the intricacies of sourcing parts for such a venerable machine thwarted their efforts.

Months stretched into an eternity, and sadly, fate took a somber turn as news arrived of the owner's passing. With no one to claim the Cadillac, it became a forgotten relic, relegated to the periphery of the workshop's domain. Neglected and exposed to the elements, the once-proud vehicle bore witness to the relentless march of decay. Its once vibrant paint dulled, giving way to the insidious advance of rust.

Into this scene of neglect and abandonment strode Jhaan, a young intern brimming with curiosity and ambition. Intrigued by the forlorn Cadillac, he queried the workshop manager about its history, eager to unravel the tale behind its faded grandeur. As the manager recounted the car's journey, a spark ignited within Jhaan—an irresistible urge to breathe new life into this forgotten masterpiece.

With the manager's blessing, Jhaan embarked on a labor of love, devoting his precious free time to the Cadillac's restoration. Armed with skill, determination, and an unwavering commitment to excellence, he meticulously dismantled, repaired, and polished every inch of the vehicle. Each stroke of his hand was infused with reverence for the craftsmanship of yesteryear, as he toiled to resurrect its former splendor.

Days turned into weeks, and weeks into months, as Jhaan's dedication bore fruit. The Cadillac emerged from its cocoon of neglect, transformed into a vision of automotive perfection. Its once-tarnished chrome gleamed, its bodywork resplendent in a fresh coat of paint. Inside, the scent of fine leather mingled with the faint whisper of history, as every detail was lovingly restored to its original glory.

Word of Jhaan's miraculous feat spread like wildfire, attracting the attention of a discerning clientele with an eye for automotive excellence. Among them was a wealthy connoisseur, captivated by the Cadillac's newfound allure. In a moment of serendipity, fate intervened once more as the car changed hands, fetching a princely sum that belied its humble beginnings.

In the vast tapestry of life, there are moments when our efforts seem to vanish into the void, unnoticed and unappreciated. It's akin to rust slowly accumulating, obscuring the shine of our aspirations and dreams. In those trying times, it's easy to succumb to disillusionment, to feel as though our endeavors are futile, destined to be swallowed by the passage of time.

Yet, amidst the shadows of doubt, there exists a glimmer of hope—a quiet reassurance that perseverance will yield its own rewards. For just as iron weathers and rusts, so too does it possess the capacity for renewal. It is a lesson in patience, in resilience, in the understanding that transformation often unfolds at its own pace.

So, we steel ourselves against the tide of uncertainty, continuing to toil in the shadows, steadfast in our belief that our efforts will not go unnoticed forever. And indeed, in the fullness of time, fate smiles upon us, bestowing upon us the recognition we so earnestly sought. Our career, once stagnant and obscured, suddenly blooms into the next stage of its evolution, propelled by the acknowledgment of our labor and the affirmation of our worth.

It is a testament to the enduring power of perseverance, a reminder that even in the darkest of moments, there exists the promise of dawn. For when we weather the storms of indifference with grace and fortitude, we emerge stronger, our resolve unshaken, our potential limitless.

So, to all those who feel themselves rusting in the shadows of obscurity, take heart. Your time will come, and when it does, your transformation will be nothing short of extraordinary.

67. PREDICTING YOUR HEALTH USING AI

AI is not only transforming the workplace by enhancing productivity and efficiency but also playing a crucial role in advancing healthcare. By predicting health outcomes and facilitating early intervention, AI has the potential to significantly improve individual well-being and public health outcomes. As AI continues to evolve, its applications in various domains are likely to expand, further revolutionizing how we work and live.

Case study 1. An obese person having very few vegetables and fruits, sleep less than 5 hours, drink 0.5 liters of sugary drinks every day, leads a sedentary life, have 8 hours of screen time, drinks alcohol and smokes one cigarette per day. What are the diseases predicted for this person.

Response by ChatGPT:

For an individual with the described lifestyle—characterized by obesity, poor diet, insufficient sleep, high consumption of sugary drinks, a sedentary lifestyle, prolonged screen time, alcohol consumption, and smoking—the following health issues and diseases are highly likely to be predicted:

Cardiovascular Diseases:

Hypertension (High Blood Pressure): A combination of obesity, high sugar intake, sedentary lifestyle, and alcohol consumption can lead to elevated blood pressure.

Heart Disease: Factors like obesity, poor diet, lack of exercise, and smoking contribute to the development of coronary artery disease and other heart conditions.

Metabolic Disorders:
Type 2 Diabetes: Obesity, high sugar intake, and a sedentary lifestyle are significant risk factors for insulin resistance and the development of type 2 diabetes.

Dyslipidemia: An unhealthy diet and lack of physical activity can lead to abnormal levels of cholesterol and triglycerides in the blood.

Respiratory Issues:
Chronic Obstructive Pulmonary Disease (COPD): Smoking, even at low levels, combined with a sedentary lifestyle, can contribute to respiratory problems including COPD.

Gastrointestinal Problems:
Non-alcoholic Fatty Liver Disease (NAFLD): Obesity and high sugar intake can lead to the accumulation of fat in the liver, resulting in NAFLD.

Gastroesophageal Reflux Disease (GERD): Obesity and poor dietary habits can increase the risk of GERD.

Musculoskeletal Disorders:
Osteoarthritis: Obesity places extra stress on joints, particularly the knees, leading to osteoarthritis.

Lower Back Pain: A sedentary lifestyle and excess weight can contribute to chronic lower back pain.

Mental Health Issues:
Depression and Anxiety: Poor sleep, prolonged screen time, and unhealthy lifestyle choices can negatively impact mental health, leading to conditions like depression and anxiety.

Sleep Disorders:
Obstructive Sleep Apnea: Obesity is a major risk factor for sleep apnea, a condition where breathing repeatedly stops and starts during sleep.

Cancer:
Increased Risk of Certain Cancers: Obesity, poor diet, alcohol consumption, and smoking can increase the risk of various cancers, including colorectal, breast, and lung cancer.

Alcohol-related Disorders:

Alcohol Use Disorder: Regular alcohol consumption can lead to dependency and associated health issues such as liver damage, cardiovascular problems, and an increased risk of certain cancers.

General Health Concerns:
Chronic Inflammation: Poor lifestyle choices can lead to chronic low-grade inflammation, which is a risk factor for various chronic diseases.

Weakened Immune System: An unhealthy diet and lifestyle can compromise the immune system, making the individual more susceptible to infections and illnesses.

To mitigate these risks, it is crucial for the individual to make significant lifestyle changes. These could include adopting a balanced diet rich in fruits and vegetables, increasing physical activity, reducing sugar and alcohol intake, quitting smoking, improving sleep hygiene, and managing screen time effectively. Regular medical check-ups and consultations with healthcare professionals can also help in monitoring health and preventing the onset of these diseases.

If you provide ChatGPT with details about your diet and lifestyle, it can predict potential diseases you might be at risk for.

68. THE SURPRISE AT THE BATTLEFIELD

Contrary to popular belief, the life of a lion in the African plains is exceptionally tough. In the wild, lions typically live for only 10-12 years, facing numerous challenges that test their resilience and survival skills. Their social structure is intricate, characterized by a complex hierarchy within the pride. Lions hunt as a group, utilizing teamwork to bring down large prey. However, once a male lion is ejected from the pride, he must fend for himself, often facing a harsh and solitary existence.

In one particular instance, a pride of lions moved into a new territory teeming with an abundance of cape buffaloes, hippopotamuses, and wildebeests. The lions, confident in their status as apex predators, assumed that their new environment would provide easy hunting and a comfortable life. However, they soon encountered unexpected resistance.

When the lions attempted to hunt the cape buffaloes, they were met with fierce retaliation. The buffaloes, using their powerful horns, charged back at the lions with incredible force. Some of the lions suffered severe abdominal injuries from the sharp horns, while others were thrown into the air, resulting in spinal injuries.

The hippopotamuses proved to be equally formidable. Known for their aggressive nature, a single bite from a hippopotamus's massive tusks could mutilate a lion's face, rendering it incapacitated or dead.

Within a matter of days, the entire pride suffered devastating losses. The combination of injuries inflicted by the buffaloes and hippopotamuses led to the pride's rapid decline, ultimately resulting in their demise. This tragic event underscores the harsh reality of life on the African plains, where even the mightiest predators can fall victim to the unforgiving nature of their environment.

Similarly, the experience of some multinational companies entering new markets mirrors the harsh realities faced by lions in new territories. These global corporations often assume that local companies will quickly capitulate, allowing them to dominate the market within a few years. However, this overconfidence can lead to unexpected challenges.

Local companies, much like the native wildlife of the African plains, possess an intimate understanding of their environment. They are well-versed in the unique cultural, economic, and regulatory landscapes of their regions. This deep-rooted knowledge allows them to employ strategies and tactics that can effectively counter the advances of multinational corporations.

In many cases, these local businesses not only withstand the initial onslaught of the global giants but also thrive by leveraging their home-field advantage. They can adapt swiftly to market changes, capitalize on local consumer preferences, and navigate regulatory frameworks with ease. Furthermore, local companies often enjoy strong brand loyalty and community support, which can be critical in maintaining their market position.

There are numerous instances where local firms have not only defended their turf but have also gone on the offensive. They innovate rapidly, enhance their product offerings, and improve customer service to outmaneuver their multinational rivals. In some scenarios, local companies grow so robust that they turn the tables and acquire the very global players that once sought to dominate them.

This dynamic underscores a fundamental lesson for multinational corporations: entering a new market requires more than just financial muscle and brand recognition. It demands a deep understanding of local nuances and a respect for the competitive capabilities of indigenous companies. The failure to recognize and adapt to these realities can lead to significant setbacks, just as the mighty lions faced defeat at the hands of the formidable buffaloes and hippopotamuses in the African wilderness.

69. YOUR WORK TOUCH MANY LIVES THAT YOU ARE NOT AWARE

Nestled within the embrace of towering trees in the heart of the forest, a solitary wildflower graced a sun-dappled meadow, its delicate petals unfurling with the arrival of spring. Yet, despite its radiant bloom, a profound sense of melancholy lingered, for there were no eyes to behold its splendor.

In this secluded haven, the wildflowers were custodians of nature's bounty, their blossoms teeming with nectar and pollen. As the warm breath of spring swept through the meadow, a symphony of buzzing heralded the arrival of honey bees, drawn by the promise of sustenance. With diligent fervor, they gathered the golden treasure and bore it aloft, traversing the verdant expanse to a distant village nestled among the hills.

In the village, the apiarists awaited the return of their industrious winged companions, for the honey they harvested was not merely a sweet indulgence but a vital source of livelihood. With meticulous care, they tended to their hives, savoring the fruits of their labor and sharing the surplus with eager patrons.

Yet, the significance of these bees transcended mere honey production. As they flitted from flower to flower, they carried with them the essence of life, bestowing upon the wildflowers the gift of pollination. In this symbiotic dance, the plants flourished, their genetic integrity preserved by the diligent ministrations of their winged allies.

The honey bees also pollinated the meadows of the villages. The stability of the plants' genetic makeup owed its gratitude to the robust health of their seeds, a testament to the flourishing ecosystem nurtured by the meadow's embrace. These seeds, imbued with vitality and resilience, ensured the perpetuation of life's intricate patterns, each delicate bloom a testament to the enduring legacy of nature's wisdom. Grazing peacefully upon the lush pasturelands, the cows provided sustenance to the villagers in the form of nourishing milk.

Moreover, the interconnected web of life extended beyond the meadow, intertwining with the fate of the nearby trees. Guided by instinct, the bees alighted upon their boughs, transferring the vital pollen that would ensure their continued growth and propagation.

Beyond their aesthetic allure, the wild flowering plants played a pivotal role as a vital source of sustenance for the diverse array of wild creatures that inhabited the surrounding expanse. From the smallest insects to the grandest of beasts, each found solace and nourishment amidst the vibrant blooms that adorned the meadow.

At times, a sense of solitude pervades, casting a pall over the routine of daily life, leaving one to ponder the seeming insignificance of their existence. Days blur into one another, each one seemingly devoid of purpose or impact, as the monotony of the daily grind threatens to envelop the spirit in its suffocating embrace.

In these moments of introspection, it's easy to succumb to the belief that one's efforts are in vain, that the work they tirelessly pursue fails to make a meaningful difference in the grand tapestry of existence. Yet, beneath the veil of self-doubt lies a truth far more profound and uplifting.

For every task undertaken, every endeavor pursued, has the potential to touch lives in ways unforeseen and profound. Like ripples upon the surface of a tranquil pond, the effects of our actions reverberate far beyond the confines of our immediate perception, shaping the world in ways both subtle and profound.

Perhaps it's the kind word spoken in passing that brings solace to a troubled heart, or the small act of kindness that brightens the day of a stranger in need. In these seemingly insignificant moments lies the true essence of our impact, for it's often in the quiet whispers of compassion and empathy that lives are touched and hearts are uplifted.

Moreover, the reach of our influence extends far beyond the boundaries of our immediate surroundings. In the interconnected web of human experience, our actions send forth tendrils of influence that stretch across vast distances, touching the lives of individuals we may never meet or even be aware of.

So, when doubt creeps in and loneliness threatens to overshadow the light within, remember this: your work, no matter how seemingly insignificant, has the power to touch lives in ways you may never know. For in the quiet moments of reflection, it's often the smallest acts of kindness that resonate most deeply with the human soul, illuminating the path forward with hope and purpose.

70. TAKING THE INITIATIVE

Attending prestigious universities or securing positions at renowned corporations can indeed be seen as significant achievements, reflecting years of dedication and hard work. However, the true measure of one's impact lies not solely in the prestige of their alma mater or the name of their employer, but rather in the actions they take and the initiatives they champion.

A degree from an Ivy League institution or a role at a Fortune 500 company may open doors and provide opportunities, but it's the individual's drive and initiative that determine their success and influence. Merely possessing a prestigious education or a high-profile job title does not inherently inspire others or bring about change. It's the proactive pursuit of knowledge, the willingness to challenge the status quo, and the relentless pursuit of improvement that truly leave a mark on the world.

Take the case of Thomas Edison, a quintessential self-learner who defied the traditional path of formal education. Despite lacking a conventional schooling background, Edison's insatiable curiosity and relentless drive led him to become one of history's most prolific inventors.

By taking initiative and embarking on numerous projects, Edison revolutionized multiple industries with his groundbreaking inventions. From the phonograph to the electric light bulb, his creations not only transformed the way people lived and worked but also propelled technological advancements that reverberated globally.

Edison's innovations didn't just ease labor; they reshaped entire economies. His inventions powered industries, created job opportunities, and spurred economic growth, ultimately contributing to the prosperity and reputation of his country.

His journey exemplifies how individual initiative, coupled with a thirst for knowledge and a determination to make a difference, can lead to monumental achievements that transcend personal success and leave a lasting legacy for generations to come. Edison's story serves as a testament to the power of self-learning and initiative in shaping the course of history.

In today's rapidly evolving landscape, those who rest complacently on the laurels of their education or job title risk fading into irrelevance. The true measure of impact lies in the ability to seize opportunities, push boundaries, and effect positive change. Whether through entrepreneurial ventures, philanthropic endeavors, or advocacy initiatives, it is the proactive engagement and unwavering commitment to making a difference that ultimately define one's significance in the global arena. Thus, while prestigious accolades may provide a platform, it is the transformative actions undertaken with that platform that truly shape the course of history.

71. THE JUDGE

The most ubiquitous role in this world is that of a judge. In reality, everyone assumes this role, constantly evaluating and forming opinions about those around them. Whether consciously or unconsciously, we judge everyone we encounter, anywhere and everywhere.

Criticizing and judging others can sometimes become a pastime for people. This behavior, often driven by a desire to feel superior or to deflect attention from one's own shortcomings, can be damaging both to those being judged and to the person doing the judging. When individuals engage in constant criticism, they may not realize the negative impact it has on their relationships and their own mental well-being.

We judge people based on their actions—whether they do good or fall short of our expectations. Our judgments extend to how people interact with us, scrutinizing their words and behavior. If someone speaks to us, we assess the tone and content of their conversation. If they remain silent, we analyze their reasons for not engaging. These evaluations are not limited to mere social interactions; they permeate every facet of our daily lives.

We often judge people based on a range of attributes, including their color, religion, gender, education, nationality, and occupation. Additionally, subtle cues such as their smile and facial expressions can influence our perceptions and assumptions. These judgments, whether conscious or unconscious, shape our interactions and can reinforce stereotypes and biases. Recognizing this tendency is the first step towards fostering a more inclusive and empathetic society, where individuals are valued for their unique qualities rather than superficial characteristics.

Our social connections are deeply influenced by our judgments. We choose friends based on our perceptions of their character and actions. Sometimes, even if someone does not seem to like us, we might still desire their friendship, influenced by our assessment of their qualities and the potential value they could bring into our lives. This constant evaluation shapes not only our personal relationships but also our professional interactions.

In the professional realm, our judgments play a crucial role in determining how we engage with clients and colleagues. We assess the worth of our services and set fees based on how we judge our clients. This judgment is influenced by their behavior, reliability, and the perceived mutual benefit of the relationship. Our professional success often hinges on these judgments, as they inform our decisions and strategies.

Our tendency to judge extends into the political sphere as well. We often vote for or choose our politicians based on their appearance and oratory skills. In many cases, the decisions we make in the political arena are heavily influenced by the superficial traits of candidates, rather than their policies or qualifications.

Appearance plays a significant role in shaping our perceptions of political figures. A well-groomed, confident-looking candidate can instill a sense of trust and reliability, even if we know little about their actual capabilities or political stance. This phenomenon, known as the "halo effect," can lead us to attribute positive qualities to someone based solely on their physical appearance.

Equally important is the way politicians speak. Eloquence, charisma, and the ability to communicate effectively can greatly impact our voting choices. A candidate who speaks with confidence, clarity, and conviction can inspire and persuade voters, often more than the content of their message itself. The power of rhetoric can sway public opinion, making a compelling speaker appear more competent and appealing.

These factors combine to create a powerful influence on our political decisions. While informed voters might consider policies, past performance, and future plans, many are swayed by the immediate impression a candidate makes. This reliance on appearance and speech can sometimes overshadow critical evaluation of a candidate's qualifications and suitability for office.

Understanding this dynamic is crucial for both voters and political candidates. Voters need to be aware of these biases and strive to look beyond superficial traits, focusing on substantive issues that affect governance and policy. Meanwhile, candidates must recognize the importance of presentation and communication in their campaigns, using these tools responsibly to engage with the electorate.

In a world where media and public image play an ever-growing role, the way politicians look and speak will continue to be a significant factor in electoral outcomes. However, fostering a more informed and discerning electorate can help ensure that our choices are based on a deeper understanding of the issues at hand and the true capabilities of those we elect to lead.

In essence, being a judge is an intrinsic part of human nature. We continuously interpret and evaluate the world around us, shaping our relationships and interactions through our judgments. This perpetual state of evaluation influences our personal choices, professional dealings, and ultimately, the fabric of our society.

72. CULTIVATING PERSONAL GROWTH

In a quaint corner of his backyard, Eddy decided to embark on a new venture: cultivating grape vines. Despite his lack of prior experience, he poured his energy into nurturing the young plants, tending to them with care and patience.

Three summers passed, and finally, Eddy's efforts bore fruit—literally. The vines yielded a modest harvest, a testament to Eddy's determination and the resilience of nature.

One sunny afternoon, Eddy's longtime friend, Mike, paid him a surprise visit. As an experienced agriculturist with a wealth of knowledge in grape cultivation, Mike couldn't help but scrutinize Eddy's handiwork. What he saw surprised him. While the vines showed promise, they were in dire need of intervention.

With a sense of urgency, Mike set to work, wielding Eddy's garden tools with practiced precision. He pruned away the excess foliage, allowing the burgeoning fruits ample space to flourish. Mike also got rid of the smaller bunch of grapes so that the larger ones got enough nutrients. Recognizing the threat of fungal diseases looming over the vineyard, Mike wasted no time in advising Eddy to apply a protective fungicide—a crucial step in safeguarding the harvest.

But Mike's expertise didn't end there. Concerned about the impending threat of avian invaders eyeing Eddy's ripening grapes, he swiftly guided his friend to procure sturdy netting. With this simple yet effective solution in place, the precious fruits would be shielded from the greedy beaks of birds eager for an easy feast.

Under Mike's guidance, Eddy's humble backyard vineyard underwent a transformation. What began as a novice's endeavor evolved into a thriving garden, brimming with potential and promise. And as the seasons cycled and the grapes ripened, Eddy couldn't help but marvel at the unexpected bounty that flourished under the watchful eye of a seasoned expert.

Just as a vintner meticulously tends to their grapevines, nurturing them with care and attention to yield the finest harvest, so too must we tend to our own personal growth. Like the delicate process of pruning grapevines to encourage optimal fruit production, we must trim away the excess in our lives and focus on the essential elements that contribute to our development.

As we embark on our journey of personal growth, it's crucial to acknowledge the multitude of factors that contribute to our overall well-being and development. From the nourishment we provide our bodies through food and drink to the activities we engage in to maintain physical fitness, each choice shapes the trajectory of our growth. Similarly, the content we consume and the relationships we cultivate play pivotal roles in influencing our path forward. Surrounding ourselves with supportive individuals who both inspire and challenge us can serve as powerful catalysts for self-improvement.

However, amid the whirlwind of distractions clamoring for our attention, it's all too easy to lose sight of our priorities. Succumbing to trivial matters can impede our progress and hinder our ability to reach our full potential. Just as a grapevine requires periodic pruning to flourish, so too must we undergo periods of introspection and refinement. By intentionally shedding excess baggage—whether it be harmful habits, negative influences, or unproductive mindsets—we create space for growth and transformation to take root.

Indeed, negative thoughts have the potential to act as formidable barriers to personal growth, stemming from past experiences and haunting our present endeavors. Therefore, it becomes imperative to cultivate a mindset brimming with positivity and optimism. By nurturing positive thoughts, we foster an environment conducive to growth and development, empowering us to overcome challenges with resilience and determination. Rather than allowing negativity to hold us back, we can redirect our focus towards the abundance of opportunities that surround us, fueling our aspirations and igniting our passion for growth.

Moreover, cultivating positive thoughts not only enhances our individual well-being but also inspires those around us to adopt a similar outlook. Through acts of kindness, gratitude, and self-affirmation, we sow the seeds of positivity, nurturing a culture that uplifts and supports others on their own journeys toward personal growth.

In essence, our pursuit of personal development mirrors the meticulous care required to tend a vineyard. It demands unwavering dedication, patience, and a discerning eye to discern what requires nurturing and what needs pruning. Like a vintner attending to each vine with precision, we must approach our own growth with equal attentiveness and intentionality. Only by cultivating our personal growth with diligence and purpose can we unlock the full depth of our potential and flourish in the richness of our aspirations, creating a ripple effect of positivity that enriches the lives of those around us.

73. LONGEVITY OF AN ACCOMPLISHMENT

How long can you celebrate your success? Accomplishments are significant milestones, but their celebration has a limited lifespan. Typically, you can revel in your achievements for about a week. After that, people tend to lose interest, and continuing to narrate your success often results in boredom and disinterest among your audience.

Accomplishments mark progress along your journey, but they are not the end goal. They serve as indicators of your hard work, dedication, and skill, but they should not be seen as final destinations. Instead, think of them as waypoints guiding you towards continuous growth and improvement.

While it's essential to acknowledge and celebrate your achievements, it's equally important to understand that these accomplishments are part of a larger, ongoing process. Each milestone reached should inspire you to set new goals and strive for even greater heights. This perspective ensures that you remain focused on personal and professional development rather than becoming complacent.

Treating accomplishments as milestones rather than endpoints fosters a mindset of lifelong learning and adaptability. In a world that is constantly evolving, the ability to stay relevant and influential depends on your willingness to embrace change and seek out new challenges. By viewing each achievement as a stepping stone, you position yourself to keep moving forward, always ready to tackle the next opportunity.

This approach also helps maintain humility and openness. Recognizing that there is always more to learn and achieve keeps you grounded and receptive to feedback and new ideas. It encourages you to collaborate with others, share knowledge, and contribute to the growth of your community or organization.

Years later, when you share your accomplishments and awards with the younger generation, they often don't pay much attention. Within your organization, repeatedly bringing up past successes can give the impression that you are stuck in the past. Executives, especially younger ones, may not take you seriously as they are focused on addressing current challenges and future goals.

Understanding the longevity of an accomplishment is crucial for maintaining relevance and respect. Celebrating your success is important, but clinging to it can hinder your growth and affect how others perceive you. To sustain long-term respect and engagement, balance the recognition of past achievements with a continuous focus on current contributions and future goals. This approach not only keeps you relevant but also demonstrates your ability to adapt and thrive in ever-changing circumstances.

Ultimately, the key to lasting respect and influence lies in your ability to progress and evolve. It's important to recognize and celebrate your successes, but this should be a brief moment of acknowledgment rather than a prolonged focus. After celebrating, promptly shift your attention to new challenges and opportunities. By doing so, you demonstrate that you are not merely resting on your laurels but are committed to continual growth and contribution.

This proactive and dynamic approach signals to others that you are adaptable, forward-thinking, and dedicated to making ongoing improvements. It shows that you understand the importance of staying relevant in a rapidly changing world. Whether in a professional setting, a community role, or any other area of life, those who consistently seek new achievements and tackle fresh challenges tend to garner greater respect and admiration.

By continuously striving for excellence and innovation, you maintain a vital and respected presence in your field. This commitment to growth not only benefits you personally but also inspires and motivates those around you. Your willingness to embrace new opportunities and face emerging challenges head-on serves as a powerful example to others, encouraging a culture of continuous improvement and resilience.

In essence, lasting respect and influence are earned through a balance of celebrating past successes and actively pursuing future goals. This balanced approach ensures that your contributions remain significant and impactful, solidifying your reputation as a leader and innovator.

74. LESSER KNOWN HABITS CAN TOPPLE US

Ben had called Marco, the handyman, to fix his garage. While Marco was inspecting the property, he noticed a more pressing issue: rainwater from the gutter was seeping into the house's foundation slab. Marco immediately informed Ben of the situation, explaining that if the problem wasn't addressed promptly, it could lead to severe structural damage to the house.

Concerned about the potential damage, Ben asked Marco to fix the problem right away. Marco set to work by first identifying and sealing the holes near the slab where the water was infiltrating. He then installed new fixtures and a more effective drainage system to ensure the water from the gutter was diverted far away from the house's foundation. This solution would help protect the structural integrity of Ben's home in the long term.

It is often the small habits, such as harboring anger, nurturing hatred and vengeance, that can ultimately cause our downfall. These seemingly minor negative emotions, when left unchecked, have a tendency to accumulate over time. Anger, for instance, can cloud our judgment, leading us to make impulsive and regrettable decisions. Hatred, on the other hand, can poison our relationships and erode our sense of inner peace. Vengeance can consume and destroy us. When we allow the desire for revenge to take root in our hearts, it can lead us down a dark path, clouding our judgment and eroding our sense of compassion. The pursuit of vengeance often blinds us to the consequences of our actions, causing us to inflict pain not only on others but also on ourselves. It can transform us into something we no longer recognize, as we become consumed by bitterness and anger.

These habits act like tiny cracks in the foundation of our well-being, gradually widening until they cause significant damage. Just as a house with a weak foundation is vulnerable to collapse, our lives can be destabilized by the persistent presence of these destructive emotions. They can affect our mental and physical health, strain our relationships, and hinder our personal growth.

Recognizing and addressing these small habits is crucial. By cultivating positive habits like forgiveness, patience, and compassion, we can counteract the negative effects of anger and hatred. Just as small, positive actions can build us up, small, negative ones can bring us down. It is through mindfulness and intentional effort that we can ensure our habits contribute to our stability and growth rather than our downfall.

75. PRACTICE

Leo dreamed of pursuing long jump as his sport of choice in school. However, he initially did not make the team, falling short of the qualifying distance by just a few centimeters.

Undeterred by this setback, Leo committed himself to improving his skills. Every day after class, he could be found at the school ground, diligently practicing his jumps. His determination was unwavering; he meticulously worked on his technique, strength, and agility. Over the next six months, his hard work paid off as his performance steadily improved, achieving a commendable distance that surpassed his previous attempts.

When the tryouts came around again the following year, Leo's persistence and dedication shone through. He not only qualified for the team but also went on to dominate the competition. His remarkable improvement culminated in a victorious season, earning him the title of champion in the long jump event. Leo's journey from disappointment to triumph became an inspiring story of perseverance and hard work for his peers and the entire school.

Any job demands significant practice and the continuous development of skills. As the world evolves at an unprecedented pace, we must adapt to changes in science, technology, and weather patterns. This adaptation requires us to learn and practice new skills to remain relevant and effective in our respective fields. Key skills for the future include presentation, marketing, motivation, and management.

Staying informed about the latest trends in one's field is crucial. Regular reading and staying updated are essential to keep up with developments and innovations. Without this, one may fall behind and fail to grasp the latest advancements that could be pivotal in their career.

Every job inherently involves some degree of management. For instance, if you are a scientist or an assistant professor, there might come a day when you are appointed as the chairman of a department. In such a role, you will need the skills to motivate and manage junior professors and students effectively. Mastering departmental management can also pave the way for managing an entire university. Leading a department requires not only subject matter expertise but also the ability to inspire and guide a team towards common goals.

Similarly, a politician who successfully runs a municipality may one day have the opportunity to lead a country. Effective management at the local level builds a foundation for taking on greater responsibilities and navigating the complexities of national leadership. A politician's ability to manage resources, respond to community needs, and implement policies at the municipal level can translate into broader governance skills necessary for national leadership.

Mastering the fundamentals of management and leadership in any role sets the stage for larger and more impactful opportunities in the future. Whether in academia, politics, business, or any other field, the ability to manage teams, projects, and resources effectively is a critical skill. Continuous learning, practice, and adaptation are the cornerstones of success in an ever-changing world.

76. UNDERCURRENTS

Raj worked diligently for a medium-sized company, consistently proving himself as the top sales representative. Every quarter, his performance outshone that of his team members, earning him recognition as the best performer. Raj's dedication was evident in his routine: he was always the first to arrive at the office and the last to leave. No task was too small for him, and he approached every job with the same level of commitment and enthusiasm.

Despite his hard work and exceptional performance, Raj found that promotions were few and far between. Years passed, and Raj realized it was time for a change. Seeking new opportunities, he enlisted the help of a consulting firm to revamp his CV, highlighting his numerous accomplishments and extensive experience.

The consulting firm helped Raj craft a compelling CV that showcased Raj's impressive track record. His achievements caught the attention of a global company, which promptly offered him the position of Senior Vice President. This new role was a testament to Raj's skills, perseverance, and the recognition he had long deserved.

In every professional setting, a complex interplay of factors distinguishes exceptional employees from their peers. These standout individuals adeptly employ strategic approaches and demonstrate effective management skills, serving as beacons of inspiration for their junior colleagues. It is widely acknowledged that behind every proficient manager lies a foundation of excellence as a skilled worker. The very strategies and techniques that propelled these individuals to prominence among their peers can be skillfully transitioned into managerial roles.

The challenges overcome while being a junior employee will one day pay rich dividends in the form of large paychecks when one is a manager due to the expertise and skills gained over time. These challenges shape future leaders, preparing them to handle greater responsibilities with confidence and competence.

Mastering and applying these proven strategies not only elevate personal performance but also foster a culture of continuous improvement within the organization. Aspiring professionals and future leaders can draw invaluable lessons from the achievements of those who have paved the way before them. By emulating their successes, they can ensure a legacy of accomplishment, innovation, and sustained progress in their careers.

In addition, these exemplary employees often serve as mentors, sharing their knowledge and experience with others. This mentorship creates a ripple effect, enhancing the overall capability and morale of the workforce. It encourages a collaborative environment where everyone is motivated to strive for excellence.

The journey from a skilled worker to a proficient manager is marked by continuous learning and adaptation. Those who excel in their roles are not only adept at navigating challenges but also at leveraging opportunities for growth. They are characterized by their resilience, strategic thinking, and unwavering commitment to their professional development.

Ultimately, the distinction between exceptional employees and their peers lies in their ability to transform challenges into opportunities, consistently deliver outstanding results, and inspire those around them. Their success stories serve as a testament to the power of hard work, strategic acumen, and the relentless pursuit of excellence. Aspiring leaders can look to these trailblazers as models of what is possible, ensuring that the path to success remains well-lit for future generations.

As professionals advance and vie for managerial positions, hiring managers meticulously assess the strategies and accomplishments that underscore leadership potential and capability. The ability to articulate significant achievements and the methodologies employed to attain them enhances one's candidacy for senior roles. Consequently, the strategic insights and management acumen developed over time not only contribute to personal success but also lay the groundwork for inspiring and guiding others within the organizational framework. By recognizing and nurturing these attributes, organizations can cultivate a robust pipeline of future leaders dedicated to driving sustained success and innovation.

77. JACK OF SEVERAL TRADES

We have inherited a vastly different world from the previous generation, one characterized by unprecedented challenges such as climate change and automation. These factors necessitate a smart and adaptive approach to professional life for both current and future generations. In this rapidly evolving landscape, continuous education has become the norm. The knowledge we acquire today can quickly become outdated, making it imperative for us to stay informed about the changes happening around us. To keep pace with these changes, it is essential to regularly read trade and professional magazines and journals, which provide insights into emerging trends and the future horizons of various industries.

The rapid pace of technological advancements and industry changes often requires us to adapt and learn new skills. Jobs that are relevant today may become obsolete tomorrow, making it essential to be flexible and open to acquiring new trades and technologies. This adaptability not only helps in maintaining job security but also opens up new career opportunities.

The swift pace of technological advancements means that industries can either thrive or collapse, significantly impacting the job market. This volatility extends to the stock market and our personal finances, underscoring the importance of financial literacy.

Effectively managing our finances requires a keen awareness of the latest industry trends. Staying informed through continuous learning and maintaining a robust reading habit is crucial for making well-informed financial decisions. Without adequate knowledge, we risk falling behind in our ability to navigate the complexities of the modern economy.

In addition to staying informed about industry trends, it's important to be aware of the housing market at different stages of our lives. Sometimes, career opportunities necessitate relocating to a new area, and understanding the housing market in potential new locations can significantly impact our financial well-being. Being knowledgeable about factors such as housing prices, rental rates, and real estate trends can help us make smarter decisions when moving for a new job.

In conclusion, embracing a mindset of lifelong learning and adaptability is essential in today's world. By keeping up with the latest developments in our fields and being prepared to pivot when necessary, we can better manage our careers and finances amidst the uncertainties of a rapidly changing world. Continuous education, staying informed about industry and housing trends, and being flexible in acquiring new skills are all key components to thriving in this dynamic environment. By integrating these practices into our daily lives, we can build resilient careers and secure financial stability, ensuring that we are well-equipped to handle the challenges and opportunities of the future.

78. CALMING THE STORMS IN OUR LIVES

Then he got into the boat and his disciples followed him.
Without warning, a furious storm came up on the lake, so that the waves swept over the boat. But Jesus was sleeping.
The disciples went and woke him, saying, "Lord, save us! We're going to drown!"
He replied, "You of little faith, why are you so afraid?" Then he got up and rebuked the winds and the waves, and it was completely calm.
The men were amazed and asked, "What kind of man is this? Even the winds and the waves obey him!" - Matthew 8:23-27.

There are times in our lives when we face overwhelming challenges and feel as if we are about to be overcome by the storms of life. In those moments, it is natural to wonder, "Where is God?" However, just as Jesus was with his disciples in the boat, God is always with us. Even when He seems silent or distant, His presence is steadfast, and His power to bring peace into our chaos is unmatched. Our faith in His presence and power can transform our fear into awe and trust.

In the parable of the sower, Jesus teaches a profound lesson about faith and how it grows in our lives. He tells of a sower who went out to sow seeds. As he scattered the seeds, some fell along the path, and the birds came and ate them up. Some fell on rocky places where they did not have much soil. They sprang up quickly, but because the soil was shallow, the plants were scorched by the sun and withered because they had no root. Other seeds fell among thorns, which grew up and choked the plants. But some seeds fell on good soil, where they produced a crop—a hundred, sixty, or thirty times what was sown.

Jesus explains that the seeds represent the word of God, and the different types of soil represent the different responses people have to that word. The seeds that fell on good soil represent those who hear the word and understand it. They have rich faith and produce a bountiful harvest. On the other hand, the seeds that fell among thorns represent those who hear the word, but the worries of this life and the deceitfulness of wealth choke the word, making it unfruitful.

Jesus compares rich faith to the seeds that fell on good ground. These seeds grow and flourish, symbolizing a faith that is deeply rooted and able to withstand challenges, producing abundant spiritual fruit. This is the kind of faith that brings forth love, joy, peace, patience, kindness, goodness, faithfulness, gentleness, and self-control.

Conversely, if we do not have faith, we are like the seeds that fell among the thorny bushes.

These seeds may start to grow, but they are soon overwhelmed by the thorns, which symbolize the distractions and worries of life, as well as the lure of wealth and material possessions. These concerns can choke our faith, preventing it from growing and bearing fruit.

To cultivate a rich faith, we must ensure that our hearts are like the good soil—open, receptive, and free from the thorns of worldly anxieties and temptations. This requires regular nurturing through prayer, reading the Scriptures, and living out God's teachings in our daily lives. By doing so, we allow God's word to take root deeply within us, enabling our faith to grow strong and produce a plentiful harvest.

79. REPENTANCE AND RENEWAL AT EASTER

The New Testament opens with the powerful proclamation of St. John the Baptist, emphasizing the imperative need for repentance as a fundamental step towards spiritual growth and reconciliation with our Creator. Just as the seasons change and our priorities evolve every decade, our spiritual journey demands a constant reevaluation of our wishes, needs, and priorities. We often find ourselves relentlessly pursuing these desires, sometimes straying from the righteous path in our fervor to attain them.

Sin is depicted as a deep trench, and acts as a formidable barrier between us and our Creator, hindering the flow of blessings into our lives. However, through genuine repentance, we bridge this chasm and restore the channels of spiritual growth and divine favor. This transformative process allows us to realign ourselves with our higher purpose and nurture our spiritual development.

A poignant example of the redemptive power of repentance is exemplified in the narrative of Christ's crucifixion. Amidst the agony of the cross, a repentant thief humbly seeks forgiveness, embodying the essence of transformation and redemption. Despite his past transgressions, his sincere repentance secures his place in the promise of paradise, highlighting the boundless mercy and grace of the Divine.

Indeed, within the rich tapestry of biblical narratives, repentance emerges as a recurring theme, underscoring its pivotal role in the spiritual journey. It is a universal invitation extended to all, regardless of past deeds or status. The story of Judas, often contemplated by theologians, serves as a sobering reminder of the potential consequences of refusing this invitation. Had he chosen the path of repentance, his destiny might have been drastically different, perhaps even ascending to the esteemed position of the first pope.

Easter and repentance are intrinsically intertwined, as both underscore the fundamental principles of redemption and renewal. We are beckoned to heed the call of repentance—to examine our hearts, reconcile with God and others, and embrace the promise of a fresh start. It is through this profound act of repentance that the true essence of Easter is realized—a celebration of hope, forgiveness, and the limitless potential for spiritual transformation.

80. THE SANTA CLAUS

In my early years, the enchantment of Christmas was wrapped in the belief in Santa Claus. The anticipation of discovering the treasures beneath our Christmas tree on that special morning filled my siblings and me with excitement. Each unwrapped gift brought forth the cherished toys I had fervently wished for, creating memories etched in the joy of those magical moments.

During those childhood years, the tradition of leaving cookies and milk on the table before bedtime added to the allure. Witnessing the disappearance of the treats on Christmas morning, accompanied by the faint chime of a bell from the attic, was a delightful confirmation that Santa had made his annual visit, spreading joy to the well-behaved children in our neighborhood.

As the passage of time carried me into adolescence, the realization that Santa was a charming tale rather than a tangible figure became evident. However, the essence of Christmas remained, evolving into a celebration of togetherness and the joy of giving.

Years later, I found myself navigating the bustling streets of the city for my first job. In the days leading up to Christmas, my focus shifted to selecting the perfect gifts for my nephews and nieces. Observing others in the midst of the same joyful pursuit, their car trunks brimming with carefully chosen presents, stirred a profound contemplation.

Seated in my car, surrounded by the holiday bustle, I found myself reflecting on the true nature of Santa Claus. It was then that I glanced into the rearview mirror and beheld a transformative revelation. Instead of my own reflection, I saw the face of Santa staring back at me.

In that moment of realization, it dawned on me: I am Santa Claus. In the symphony of adults preparing and exchanging gifts during the Christmas season, each car trunk laden with surprises became a modern sleigh. The magic of Santa, once perceived as a whimsical tale, now lived within the spirit of every adult, radiating joy and embodying the true meaning of Christmas.

Ho...Ho... Ho. Merry Christmas.

www.ingramcontent.com/pod-product-compliance
Lightning Source LLC
Chambersburg PA
CBHW072343090426
42741CB00012B/2907